Aikido
and Words of Power

The Sacred Sounds of Kototama

William Gleason

Destiny Books
Rochester, Vermont

Destiny Books
One Park Street
Rochester, Vermont 05767
www.DestinyBooks.com

Destiny Books is a division of Inner Traditions International

Library of Congress Cataloging-in-Publication Data
Gleason, William, 1943–
  Aikido and words of power : the sacred sounds of Kototama / William Gleason.
     p. cm.
  Includes bibliographical references and index.
  ISBN 978-1-59477-245-0 (pbk.)
  1. Aikido. 2. Aikido—Psychological aspects. I. Title.
  GV1114.35.G53 2009
  796.815'4—dc22

                                                                        2008040653

Printed and bound in Canada by Transcontinental Printing

10 9 8 7 6 5 4 3 2 1

Illustrations by Gareth Hinds
Calligraphy by Kazuaki Tanahashi
Watercolor paintings by Daniel doAmaral
Photographs of technical demonstrations by Roy Katalan
Ukemi for technical demonstration photos by Jay Weik, Steven Rust, Gordon Fontaine, and
    Josh Puskarich
Figure 1.9 on page 41 from Koji Ogasawara, *Kototama Hyakushin* (Tokyo: Toyokan, 1969), 56
Figure 2.1 on page 61 by Katsumi Sugita
Figure 2.2 on page 64 from Matsuzo Hamamoto, *Bansei Ikkei no Genri to Hanya Shingo no
    Nazo* (Tokyo: Kasumigaseki, 1948), 211
Figure 4.31 on page 169 by Cynthia Zoppa

Text design and layout by Jon Desautels
This book was typeset in Garamond Premier Pro with Hiroshige and Zapf Humanist used as display typefaces

To send correspondence to the author of this book, mail a first-class letter to the author c/o Inner Traditions • Bear & Company, One Park Street, Rochester, VT 05767, and we will forward the communication.

Dedicated to the teachers who truly changed my life.

■

Michio Kushi

Seigo Yamaguchi

Sanae Odano

Mitsugi Saotome

■

■ *Morihei Ueshiba with katana*

CONTENTS

FOREWORD

Bill Gleason sensei has trained and researched Aikido for many years and is now publishing his second book on Aikido. I feel privileged that he is sharing the result of his many years of training with us, and I am certain that this latest work will be a great guide for those pursuing the practice of Aikido.

Gleason sensei and I are comrades in Aikido, having begun our studies at about the same age and approximately the same time. We met as young men at Honbu Dojo in Tokyo, some forty years ago. Since we were training every day, we took for granted what I now consider a golden age in Aikido; the dojo was vibrant with the energy of many great shihan who had been direct students of O-sensei. What a remarkable time!

We and others of our generation, including our friends Mary Heiny of the United States and Christian Tissier of France, now both highly regarded sensei, had an unparalleled opportunity to receive the instruction of O-sensei's students—Doshu Kisshomaru Ueshiba sensei, Osawa sensei, Okumura sensei, Koichi Tohei sensei, Yamaguchi sensei, Saotome sensei, and Arikawa sensei, among others.

Gleason sensei especially trained with Seigo Yamaguchi sensei and Mitsugi Saotome sensei. With their influence as a foundation, Gleason sensei has, over the past forty years, transformed his Aikido beyond the elementary execution of technique to an art that is an expression of his heart.

Gleason sensei continues to research and refine his study of all aspects of Aikido—philosophical, physical, and spiritual, intertwined as they are. We are fortunate that he has undertaken this second book, which is imbued with his unique Aikido experience.

Hiroshi Ikeda shihan
Aikido seventh dan
Aikido Schools of Ueshiba (ASU)

SHOBU AIKIDO SEISHIN

SHIN (MAKOTO) - SINCERITY, HONESTY, AND REALITY ARE THE THREE VIRTUES SYMBOLIZED BY THE MIRROR. THEY ARE REALIZED THROUGH THE QUALITY OF OUR TRAINING AND THROUGH SELF-REFLECTION. EACH IS A CHECKPOINT FOR THE OTHER AND CAN ONLY EXIST AS THE TOTALITY OF SHIN OR MAKOTO.

ZEN - VIRTUE DEPENDS ON THE SWORD OF JUDGMENT AND COURAGE WHICH CAN GIVE LIFE OR TAKE IT AWAY. THE COMBINATION OF THESE TWO FACTORS PRODUCES TRUE VIRTUE BEYOND RIGHT AND WRONG OR GOOD AND BAD. WHEN BOTH ARE PRESENT AND BALANCED THE RESULT IS OMOIYARI, MUTUAL CONSIDERATION FOR OTHERS.

BI - BEAUTY IS THE JEWEL OF HUMAN LIFE WHICH ENSUES FROM A FEELING OF MAGNANIMITY TOWARDS OTHERS AND THE FLEXIBILITY TO RESOLVE CONFLICTS WITHOUT ANGER OR THE NEED TO WIN.

AI - LOVE AND HARMONY ARE THE QUALITIES OF GREATNESS AND LEADERSHIP WHICH COME OUT OF SELFLESS COMPASSION FOR OTHERS. THIS IS THE ESSENCE OF AIKIDO.

TI - WISDOM AND CONTROL. TO CONTROL OURSELVES REQUIRES THE SENSITIVITY OF INTUITIVE WISDOM. THIS IS THE VIRTUE OF UPRIGHTNESS AND SPIRITUAL ENLIGHTENMENT.

■ *Shobu Aikido Seishin plaque*

SHOBU GOHO:
THE FIVE PRINCIPLES OF AIKIDO

Shin is *makoto,* the clear mirror of beginner's mind; sincerity, with no hidden agenda. This is *reitai ittai,* body and spirit as one. It is called *naohi,* our direct spirit, or *iku tama,* the spirit of life. The word *shin* means "core" or "essence." It also can mean both "God" and "faith." This is the essence of human life. This is the *kototama* of U and Su, which are also represented by the deities Uhijini no kami and Suhijini no kami.

Zen is virtue. Real virtue is always invisible. It is the sword of judgment and courage, the spirit of Aratama. In Buddhism it may be likened to the Bodhisattva Manjusri—the ki of fire, which comes forth as compassion for the world. This is the kototama of E and Re, represented by Tsunugui no kami and Ikugui no kami, the deities that tie the ki of life together.

Bi is beauty, the jewel of human life. Lacking love and beauty, the water ki of Nigitama is already dead. Nigitama comes forth as love, mercy, and magnanimity toward others. It creates the power and flexibility to resolve conflicts without anger or the need to win. When Nigitama is strong, our physical health is strong and abundant. In Buddhism it may be likened to the Bodhisattva Kannon, which hears the cries of the world and responds immediately. In Shinto it is the deity Toyokumo no kami, the kototama of O.

Ai is both love and harmony, the spirit that embraces all things equally. It is consciousness, the life force itself. It is the quality of greatness and leadership, the soul of Sakitama, the spirit of prosperity. In Shinto this is called Kuni toko tachi no kami, the deity that continually establishes the material world.

Chi is the fullness of ki, which manifests as unifying wisdom, the essence of enlightenment. This is the foundation of uprightness and spiritual consciousness. In Buddhism it represents the vehicle of Buddha, the fully enlightened one. It is the ancestor of Kushitama, the kototama of I and Gi. These kototama are also likened to the deities Ohotonoji no kami and Ohotonobe no kami.

AMATSU SYLLABARIES

THE FIFTY-SOUNDS TABLE SHOWN IN
THREE DIFFERENT ORDERS

Amatsu Kanagi

WA	RA	YA	MA	HA	NA	TA	SA	KA	A
WI	RI	YI	MI	HI	NI	TI	SI	KI	I
WU	RU	YU	MU	HU	NU	TU	SU	KU	U
WE	RE	YE	ME	HE	NE	TE	SE	KE	E
WO	RO	YO	MO	HO	NO	TO	SO	KO	O

Amatsu Sugaso

WA	NA	RA	MA	YA	HA	SA	KA	TA	A
WO	NO	RO	MO	YO	HO	SO	KO	TO	O
WU	NU	RU	MU	YU	HU	SU	KU	TU	U
WE	NE	RE	ME	YE	HE	SE	KE	TE	E
WI	NI	RI	MI	YI	HI	SI	KI	TI	I

Amatsu Futonorito

WA	SA	YA	NA	RA	HA	MA	KA	TA	A
WI	SI	YI	NI	RI	HI	MI	KI	TI	I
WE	SE	YE	NE	RE	HE	ME	KE	TE	E
WO	SO	YO	NO	RO	HO	MO	KO	TO	O
WU	SU	YU	NU	RU	HU	MU	KU	TU	U

A NOTE ABOUT PRONUNCIATION

Pronunciation of the Kototama Syllables

A   is pronounced as in *father*.

E   is pronounced as in *ale*.

I   is pronounced as in *easy*.

O   is pronounced as in *over*.

U   is pronounced as in *cool*.

Hu is pronounced *fu*.

Si   is pronounced *shi*.

Ti   is pronounced *chi*.

Tu   is pronounced *tsu*.

Glossary

A glossary of terms used is provided at the back of the book. In some cases, foreign words and technical terms are explained in the text; in other cases, not. Readers will sometimes wish to turn to the glossary.

Iroha Uta: The song of the fifty sounds (calligraphy by Shuya Yamamoto)

INTRODUCTION

Aikido is one spirit, four souls, three origins, and eight powers. These are the words of Morihei Ueshiba O-sensei, the founder of Aikido. Although these were the teachings of the founder, their actual relevance to our training seems to have been given very little consideration since his passing in 1969. In my first book, *The Spiritual Foundations of Aikido* (SFOA), I attempted to introduce these original teachings to the West. How much success I have had is difficult to know, yet I am grateful for those who have attempted to digest and put these teachings into practice.

Since the publication of SFOA approximately twelve years ago, I have received many comments and questions on the material. The most common inquiries have been requests for further philosophical clarification and greater detail concerning the practical application of the founder's teachings.

The direct students of the founder received his spiritual and physical teachings day in and day out. Many of them lived in the dojo and took care of O-sensei's daily needs in great detail. In this way they received his influence on a very deep and personal level. Unfortunately, the necessary environment for this kind of training is difficult to create in modern Western society. It has mostly disappeared in Japan as well.

Of those students who studied directly with the founder, very few are still with us today, and even fewer are actively teaching and training new students. Each generation becomes more estranged from the true spirit of Aikido and its practical application. So often today, Aikido is being practiced merely as a repetition of physical movements. This misses its essence altogether.

Although based on some of the most ancient teachings of mankind, Aikido as it is practiced today is still a very young art. Compared to the Chinese martial arts, for example, its philosophy, principles, and spiritual value are, as of yet, largely undocumented and untaught. It is necessary, I believe, to clarify Aikido as the study of nature's movement and principle.

The founder was a man of deep spiritual conviction, the practice of which included daily meditation, chanting, and prayer, as well as the technical practice of Aikido. He was also an avid scholar of many spiritual traditions including ancient Shinto and the *kototama* (universal consciousness as the spirit of sound) on which it is based. If Aikido is going to be passed down to the next generation, I believe it will require the clarification of both O-sensei's original message and its application in daily training and daily life.

Furthermore, Aikido is an art requiring direct transmission from teacher to student. It cannot be passed down in large groups where the students are left to their own devices and interpretations. As in traditional disciplines of more ancient times, it requires personal interchange not only physically, but also psychologically and spiritually.

In order to address these various concerns, which I take very personally, I began to write *Aikido and Words of Power*. During this six-year process my own teaching has also deepened and benefited, resulting in the creation of the Shobu Okugyo, an ongoing series of advanced training sessions for the purpose of teaching Aikido as a path to spiritual realization.

In these five-day seminars, Aikido is studied as a complete discipline including daily meditation, discussion of principles, and several hours a day of on-the-mat training that directly relates to the kototama principle on which it is based. The material presented in this book has served as the basis of our study.

As in SFOA, each chapter builds on the ones preceding it, and the reader is therefore advised not to skip ahead on the first reading. Throughout the book there are quotes from Japanese teachings, most of which are previously unpublished in English. These include the teachings of Yamaguchi Shido, Deguchi Onisaburo, and Morihei Ueshiba.

The kototama teachings of Yamaguchi Shido became the source material for the work of Deguchi Onisaburo. Deguchi sensei, in turn, taught the kototama principle to Morihei Ueshiba O-sensei, the founder of Aikido. The sometimes archaic language and the repetitious nature of these writings make it difficult to quote word for word or give exact page numbers. I have therefore paraphrased these teachings and put them in italics as they appear throughout the book.

As a continuation of *The Spiritual Foundations of Aikido,* this volume introduces many new aspects of the kototama, as well as the various Shinto deities associated with them. In some cases the same kototama may have more than one representative deity. Some were names of former emperors, while others related directly to the kototama principle. This is perhaps a means of honoring great leaders, but it doesn't concern us here. This work relies mainly on the strictly symbolic arrangement of the deities in the Japanese Kojiki, the book of ancient events. For this reason, the names have been excluded from this text except where they are actually beneficial to understanding the message of this book.

One spirit and four souls are the five vowel dimensions of infinite space, the life force of the universe. The eight powers are the paired rhythms that bring forth the real aspects of the manifest world. The synchronization of these complementary-antagonistic energies creates the spark of life—the fulcrum of universal principle. It is the activity of *nakaima,* "the absolute here and now."

When the eight powers and the five dimensions are combined, the creative principle of *aiki,* or universal harmony, begins its function as actual vibration. This is called *sangen,* or the three origins. In Aikido practice these should be understood as *hi no ki,* or the ki of fire; *mizu no ki,* or the ki of water; and *tsuchi no ki,* or the ki of earth.

Chapter 2 deals with the trinity of sangen, first as the relationship between relative and absolute, and second as polarity in relation to form and movement. Tsuchi no ki is the inexhaustible origin of life; hi no ki and mizu no ki are the active elements of the triangle principle. This is *himitsu,* or the mystery of three, the interchange between relative and absolute.

The first spiritual form created from the polarity of fire and water ki is the cross of *tate* and *yoko*. The visible form of nature is created from the vertical (tate) and horizontal (yoko) ki that hides behind the manifest world as its structural and energetic foundation. This pattern should be followed in Aikido as well. Form should never be created directly; rather, it should emerge from the balance of vertical and horizontal energy. When we establish the cross as the origin and controlling factor of our movement, spiral form unfolds automatically. This is discussed in detail in chapter 2.

Chapter 3 is titled "Iki: The Breath of Life." *Iki* is the ki of the life will, the unborn ki from which universal and individual breath begin. This chapter begins with a comparison of the breath, or *kokyu*, of Heaven, Earth, and human beings. Kokyu is the first movement of principle. In Shinto, and therefore in Aikido, principle is not an abstract; it begins with the movement of mind, breath, and ki as the movement of universal body.

Kokyu is the bridge between body and spirit. In Aikido training it is the source of power, timing, and form. It is through the study of kokyu that mind and body are united and understood to be one and the same. For this reason, an entire chapter has been devoted to the breath as both form and feeling.

In Aikido form, kokyu manifests first as the forms of *misogi,* or spiritual purification. Secondly, it is integral to the hand forms of Aikido technique. Finally, it is inherent in the method of holding the body and practicing Kokyu ho, the fundamental training for ki development. From Kokyu ho, in turn, the endless varieties of Kokyu nage are born.

Chapter 4 is titled "Shugyo: The Spiritual Training of Technique." In other words, the physical training of Aikido, approached properly, is in and of itself a method of spiritual development. This should not be taken for granted, however. It should be questioned continually and approached with great respect.

Chapter 4 begins with a discussion of the various levels of Aikido training and accomplishment. It introduces the spiritual levels of *kanagi, sugaso,* and *futonorito* as the basis of *kotai, jutai, ryutai,* and *kitai* training. Proper body movement is discussed as the foundation of good technique. This begins with *hanmi,* our basic stance, and finishes with the proper use of the arms.

Chapter 4 was by far the most difficult to write. Aikido technique is an intuitive experience and cannot be captured by any amount of words or explanation. The real *aiki* is inside the body even before technique begins. It is a kind of very high-level yoga in which body and mind are in complete harmony with each other and with the ki of nature. Nevertheless, both technique and principle must be explained. If these things are not understood, the student remains forever the dutiful slave of his teacher. This is a failure of the teacher and leads to the degeneration of the art. Real development necessarily leads to freedom.

The last chapter is titled "Inochi: Aikido as a Spiritual Path." In this chapter, Aikido and the kototama principle are explored as the criteria of both physical and spiritual evolution. The path of Shinto, as well as that of esoteric Buddhism and Aikido, is a practice of embodying the spiritual ki of nature, and thereby realizing the great universal spirit as your own true nature. In the words of O-sensei, *Ware soku uchu,* "the universe and I are the same."

The practice of Aikido is not one of obtaining an abstract state of understanding or even an enlightened state of consciousness that distinguishes one from anyone else. Rather it is to grasp what it means to be truly human, and to manifest the four virtues innate in the spirit and soul. This is the main topic of chapter 5.

The book itself, rather than the introduction to the book, is the place to contemplate this material in depth, and therefore I welcome you to enter and share it with me. It is at best, however, a finger pointing to the moon. Until each person, through individual practice and realization, makes it his or her own, it is of little value.

Finally, and of extreme importance, the selfless sacrifice of time and effort made by so many people who support the dojo and help keep it going was absolutely necessary in finishing this work. There are too many to mention, yet I must introduce those directly involved in the production of the book.

Roy Katalan, a professional photographer of exceptional sensitivity, traveled from Ohio to Massachusetts to be part of this project. The original shoot included some 4,000 photographs, which he then had to edit down to about 300. Gareth Hinds, a published illustrator and student of Aikido, for the most part donated his artwork, time, and effort.

I also feel very privileged to include artwork donated by Daniel doAmaral. Daniel is my friend of some twenty-seven years and an incredibly talented artist. Additionally, the calligraphy of renowned artist Kazuaki Tanahashi gives this work a quality of refinement that could hardly be achieved through any other medium, and I want to express my gratitude for his participation.

Finally, it is of great importance to me to mention the beautiful artwork of Shuya Yamamoto that is used in the cover design of *Aikido and Words of Power*. I first met Yamamoto sensei at Honbu dojo in Japan at the beginning of my training. Today Yamamoto sensei is a teacher at the Aikido world headquarters in Tokyo, yet he also has made a lifelong study out of writing the Iroha Uta, a poem containing all the letters of the Japanese syllabary, in ancient Japanese letters.

Last but not least, I want to thank my own students for their tireless hours of physical participation in order to photograph the actual techniques of Aikido. Attempting to maintain the dynamic feeling of actual training while catching the fine points on film was a long and difficult process. My students who appear in the actual demonstrations of technique include Jay Weik, Steven Rust, Gordon Fontaine, and Josh Puskarich.

The Spirit of Universal Harmony

▪ *Aikitama*

IN THE BEGINNING—
THE KOTOTAMA OF SU

Aikido has its roots in Japanese Shinto, the original teaching of which is the *kototama*. It is from the kototama, which translates as "the souls of words," that the innate sensibilities of language and thought are created. The kototama, however, should not be seen as a tool for dividing people or distinguishing one race from another. As the root of thought itself, and therefore of all spoken language, it is a tool for understanding our common origins and ultimate unity.

The kototama is not a theory or even a teaching. It is the life energy, or *ki,* that gives birth to consciousness in all its myriad forms. In other words, it is mind that creates human beings, and not the other way around. Our uniqueness as members of the animal kingdom is our ability to translate our feelings into abstract thought, and therefore into creativity. The manner in which we use this tool largely determines the quality of our lives and even the life of our planet.

Aikitama, the spirit of harmony, is the function of the word souls; it is the creative ki of the universe. Like the fish in the great oceans, we are immersed in a sea of consciousness. So deeply immersed are we, in fact, that we cannot easily see our own nature or the decisive role that we inevitably play in the creation of our own reality. It is only when

■ *Kotoha*

■ *Kanji symbol of Su*

our subjective experience is verified by the objective principle of original mind that reality becomes consistently clear.

Kototama is "the word," which is destined to become manifest in human form. It is *kotoha,* or the super-speed invisible light wave (*koto*) vibration (*ha*) of life. As the life force of all things it is omnipresent; there is nothing outside of it. As the source of consciousness it is omniscient. As the source of movement and, therefore, power, it is omnipotent. As the reality behind appearances it is the unborn, that which knows no separation among the eternal trinity of mind, matter, and spirit.

In the words of Gautama Buddha, "Verily, there is a realm where there is neither the solid nor the fluid, neither heat nor motion, neither this world nor any other world, neither sun nor moon. . . . If there were not this Unborn, this Unoriginated, this Uncreated, this Unformed, escape from the world of the born, the originated, the created, the formed, would not be possible."[1]

The creator spirit of the universe, from which all other word souls are born, is the kototama of Su. The ki of Su is pure movement; it is the spirit of the infinite universe and our own spirit as well. It gives birth continually to U, the mechanical judgment of our five basic senses. It is through this consciousness that the world of form is first perceived. What, then, is the origin of Su?

The great origin of Su is the boundless emptiness of Mu. To merge with this consciousness is to attain the great mirror wisdom. It is to discover the clear mirror of perfect mind called *sunyata.* Seen as existence, it is emptiness. Seen as emptiness, it is existence. Out of this endless expanse the creative power of universal consciousness becomes full and ripe and comes forth as the great yang fire ki of Ho. From the movement of this great yang, the first particle of spiritual ki is born. It is called *hochi.*

This brightly shining ki radiating outward and gathering other spiritual particles of ki around it gives birth to the kototama of Su. Su, reaching out in all directions, gives birth to the kototama of U. This is the beginning of the spiritual world, the realm of intuitive mind, or *kamyo,* the age of the gods.

U dimension, born from the movement of Su, is *reitai ittai,* spirit and body as one. It is the realm of the senses, in which there is no ability to separate one thing from another. It contains no awareness of self and other. In Buddhism, it is called the Dharmakaya, the ground of being. In Buddhist terms, the word *emptiness* means the lack of any individual or separate being. In other words, it means the total interdependency of all things. The quality of emptiness is the voice of Ku. Mu, its counterpart, is the life ki that fills that great void.

■ *Reitai ittai*

Morihei Ueshiba O-sensei described *the great emptiness of being* as Su-U-Yu-Mu. Su-U is absolute and relative as one. At the center of the brain is *iwasu,* the nest of the fifty sounds. This is the island (*shima*) where sound and meaning unite. Yu is the harmonious balance of fire and water ki, yin and yang. It stands between and unites U and Mu, matter and ki. Ki and matter combined create *umu,* the power of birth. As a noun it becomes *umi,* the ocean from which physical life is born on this planet.

The kototama of Su contains and gives birth to all other dimensions of existence. Just as our individual bodies are composed of millions of cells, the kototama of Su contains all other kototama. Su is therefore called "the creator spirit of the universe." Morihei Ueshiba, the founder of Aikido, stated that the Biblical teaching, "In the beginning was the word," should be understood as the kototama of Su.

As pure movement, Su is the spirit of nonresistance. It brings our five senses to a state of peace. This is *shisuka*, the deep, quiet roaring beneath the busy-ness of our everyday minds. Within stillness is the greatest movement, yet it is void of any fixed or permanent reality. Union with this spiritual origin is the seminal meaning of the word *yoga.* Deguchi Onisaburo, O-sensei's spiritual teacher, described the process as follows:

> *First of all there is Su (*hochi*). Using all of your power you must make that great origin clear. Possessing this wisdom deep within your* hara, *your physical and psychic center, you will be able to bring your mind and senses to a state of peace, even within demanding activity. The wisdom that lies undiscovered at the center of your being must become the means through which you actually hear the teaching of Su.*
>
> *Within the infinite void, the kototama of Su ringing out brings us the great origin. Using this light of wisdom as your tool, you will come to hear the true teaching of the creator spirit of Ame no Minaka*

■ *Ame no Minaka Nushi*

Nushi. When one awakens the desire to clearly understand this infinite origin, one should proceed with great caution and humility and perform purification both morning and evening.

Fully receiving the truth and fullness of Su, swallow it completely; bring it into your hara and become one with the universe. Thereafter for three days nurture this feeling both day and night. Listen to the voice of the great void and smell the ki of vast emptiness. If you continue to train yourself in this way, regardless of the degree of genius or lack of it, you will inevitably receive the appropriate light of wisdom.

In the original Shinto, this process was called *kamigakari,* to be possessed by divine presence. The paradox here is that the spiritual ki of Ame no Minaka Nushi is your own original nature; it is the *nushi* (ruler) who resides at the center of *ame* (the heavenly realm of consciousness).

Ama, or *ame,* is Heaven. *Ama* is the infinite expansion of consciousness from which *mana,* "word souls," are born. The ki of *me* causes the cycling of that consciousness. *No* is the consciousness of Su, the five senses, extending down into the small brain to become *honno,* or instinct. This is the beginning of memory, and therefore movement of individual species. *Minaka* is the exact center, here and now, the axis of time and space. This axis of consciousness is the life will, the volition of the life force and its endless evolution.

The life will (I) and power (Wi) reside at the center of Su, within the absolute here and now. This is called *nakaima. Nu* is the materialization of *no,* and *shi* is our spiritual antennae, that which makes thought possible and thereby leads us toward spiritual awakening. The life power (Wi) is the centripetal force that holds ki inside of our hara and gives us longevity. At the center of Su, the life will and power are united by our first in breath, the fire ki of the kototama of Yi.

The kototama of Yi leads our inhalation. Drawing ki from one point—up our spine to the center of our brain—our physical body follows that ki to become upright. Drawing ki upward in this way, we create what is called in Shinto *ame no hashi date,* "the standing bridge of Heaven." In simple terms, this functions as our spiritual antennae. It may also be expressed as *shin,* which means "core," "essence," or even "god."

Standing between and unifying the seeming separation of Heaven and Earth (A-Wa), our direction becomes straight like an arrow (Ya) toward the truth of our own nature. The sound of Ya, therefore, is also expressed as "the opening of the eye of Heaven." It is the life will expanding as the ki of Ya meets itself at countless points of intersection.

In Shinto this kototama is represented by the sacred mirror of Yata in the main hall of Ise Shrine in Japan. It is the mind of the Dharmakaya, the great mirror wisdom. In Buddhism it is also expressed as the "Diamond Net of Indra," in which all things in the universe are totally interconnected and interdependent. It is the net that connects all individual existence yet exists only as a single entity.

Represented by the kototama of Ya Yi Ye Yo Yu, mankind stands between and unifies the ki of Heaven and Earth. We have no choice but to stand in the center, because that is where nature becomes conscious of itself. Awareness arises at the center of things because it is the center of all things. Because it looks in the ten directions, there is past and future, here and there, self and other. What we perceive as *out there* is *here,* at the center. Without *here* there would be no *out there;* without center there would be no recognition of anything.

The deity of the center, Ame no Minaka Nushi, resides within Taka Ama Hara, the high heavenly plane. This is the realm of A dimension's ki, the infinite expansion of compassion and spiritual prosperity. It is the essence of Su coming forth for the first time. This expanding ki gives birth to Takami musubi no kami, the deity representing the power of contrast.

In the words of Deguchi Onisaburo, *An uncountable number of infinitesimal particles of spiritual light expanding in all directions create a sphere of spiritual ki (Ma) stretched to its greatest point of tension. It is calle*d tama, *the universal soul. Attempting to release this great tension, ki begins to connect and race through the center of this sphere. This is the kototama of Ka, the motive power of spiral movement.*

The kototama of Ha is the great vitality of awareness. It reaches out to the extremities of the universe in an instant and rings forth with the sound of Ki-Ki-Ki. It is likened to the deity Omotaru no kami, who confronts all things directly and oversees them from above. Ra is

■ *Fig. 1.1. Opening of the eye of Heaven (from an original watercolor by Daniel doAmaral)*

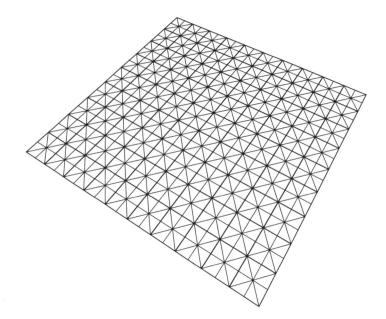

■ *Fig. 1.2. Ya-ta, ki fields merging*

■ *Taka Ama Hara*

the final act of creation. Spiraling outward it encloses and contains the entire universe—the realm of Taka Ama Hara, or high heavenly plane.

In other words, *taka* is the beginning of polarity. O-sensei used the phrase *takemusu aikido,* relating Aikido to the interchange of fire and water ki in the creative process. *Kama* means "a large cooking pot"; it is the place where the word souls, the ki of our spirit, are cooked until they become *mana,* the tools of thought. The kototama of Ka is the ki that harnesses the motive power of the life will in order to produce movement. This is *hataraki,* the life will first manifesting its creative power through A dimension's ki. The word *hataraki* is therefore abbreviated to the word *hara,* the original field of life's ki. The kototama of Ha is the creative breath of Heaven. It is the power of recognition that gives birth to *awa,* or awareness. Ra is the yang power that encompasses our awareness and creates the ability of intellect.

Taka Ama Hara, the high heavenly plane, is not only the entire universe, but also our physical hara. In our brain it is the origin of thought. In our physical body it is the electromagnetic energy field of life ki. When the brow chakra, the third eye, and *tanden no ichi,* "one point," are consciously unified, the essence of human quality—our direct, or intuitive, perception—begins.

Our one point is the place of I dimension's ki. It is *nakaima,* the absolute present, the here and now. It is the point from which *souzou,* the creation of the universe, begins. The kototama of I remains behind the scenes, working through, uniting, and controlling all the other dimensions. Within the stillness of the void, it is the subtle ki of life itself—the self-perpetuating force of evolution.

The kototama of I is the unformed human seed within the womb of Su. The advent of time-space doesn't exist without a still point, and that point begins with our own self-awareness. Lacking the ability to stand in the center, we can make no assessment or interpretation of the world.

All things that are born also die, yet the life will continually changes form and remains as the unborn. "The mind turns in accordance with the 10,000 things. The pivot on which it turns is verily hard to know."[2] I dimension's ki remains hidden like salt that has been dissolved in water.

Realizing I dimension is to stand between and unify all opposites. This is not an intellectual exercise. It requires sincere and dedicated training of body, mind, and spirit. Until our own subjective experience is verified by objective understanding, our thoughts and words can never be truly simple yet reflect reality at face value. The word *michi* means "the path of divine wisdom." More specifically it is *inochi,* or the path toward the realization of I dimension. This realization depends on developing our E dimension's capacity. It is only through the discerning wisdom of E dimension that I dimension can be experienced.

The *kanji* (ideogram) for michi, however, has several dictionary readings. It is read *sujimichi,* "the thread of pure reason"; *kotowari,* "the principle of the word"; and *michiru,* "the fullness, or abundance, of wisdom." This should not be seen, therefore, as dwelling merely in the realm of spiritual ki. Unless our intuitive judgment, our E dimension, clarifies that experience, it has no power to create a better world.

Jesus of Nazareth spoke of this quality: "You are the salt of the earth, but if salt has lost its taste, how can its saltiness by restored? It is no longer good for anything, but is thrown out and trampled under foot."[3] Human judgment and intuition today have been shrouded

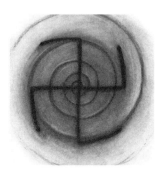

■ *Fig. 1.3. Ka—motive power within the spiral*

beneath the greed and desires of our U dimension's limited perception.

Outside of the five vowel dimensions and the eight powers of movement, there is nothing to be found. The word (or word souls) is the totality of all things in the three worlds of spirit, mind, and body. Nevertheless, within this great origin there is no separate self. This is the illusion created by human beings.

It is through E dimension's judgment capacity that we became human beings, yet it is also this same capacity through which we created the idea of a separate self and the consequent competitive world in which we live. This is the tool of human development and until it is polished and refined to a high level, we will be unable to create a truly human society.

In the words of the founder, *The kototama is not the sound of the human voice, it is the red blood boiling forth from your hara.* The fullness of the life will is the kototama of Ti. It means both "blood" and "wisdom," the fullness of body and spirit. As we draw breath into our one point and again release it, we continually replenish the circulation of our ki and the nourishment of our blood. Drawing our mind to one point, we are led toward the discovery of wisdom.

To the degree that this wisdom is realized, we are able to dwell within the vibration of Su, where the senses are at peace and the mind is free from turmoil and struggle. This is our original nature, yet we can't see it until our spiritual eyes are opened. We are swimming in the great ocean of Su, yet our limited perception cannot see it and we continue to search outside of ourselves for the truth of life.

Wherever we see spiral form, the ki of Su is strongest. This is most obvious at the main chakras of the body—our physical hara; the crown chakra at the top of the head; and the center of the palms and tips of our fingers and toes. These are earth ki, the source, or origin, of our life energy.

As mentioned above, the ki of Su brings the five senses to a state of calm and peacefulness. The ability to maintain this state in difficult times requires a much higher level of understanding than any degree of technical expertise. This is what O-sensei referred to as *agatsu,* defeating oneself. The mind of conflict appears to be ready for anything, yet it knows not the peacefulness of the origin.

In the civil wars of Japan, the samurai often had little time to perfect their fighting skills. They discovered, therefore, that the ability to remain calm in the midst of battle was often the more important factor determining one's survival. The peaceful mind has no idea how to deal with conflict; it knows neither confidence nor lack of confidence, and therefore deals in the here and now. Since it doesn't concentrate on hypothetical situations, it can be successful.

Coming from this place requires maturity of practice. When your body and mind are rooted in your one point, all of the tension in your arms and shoulders falls away. As a result, your movement becomes *subayaka,* swift and light.

■ *Fig. 1.4. Su in the human body*

By keeping your mind in your one point as you practice, you approach what Buddhism calls *emptiness functioning as the basis of daily activity.* Center yourself in your one point and drop all defensiveness and apprehension. As you gain trust in your body's innate wisdom you will be able to move freely, adapting naturally to your partner's movement, yet never losing that centeredness. In Buddhism this state of mind is shown by Kannon, the goddess of mercy with one thousand arms.

Aikido is the superlative way to practice the kototama. It is the means by which one realizes his true nature as a god and finds ultimate freedom. These powerful words of O-sensei leave little doubt as to his orientation concerning the relationship between Aikido and the kototama. Those who pursue only technique will reach neither spiritual fulfillment nor technical mastery. Aikido is a means of both realizing and manifesting

■ *Fig. 1.5. Thousand-armed Kannon*

the kototama. It is a practice designed for the realization of our own nature as universal spirit. As we gain awareness of the five dimensions of ki, our spiritual qualities and physical power come forth.

O-sensei created Aikido as a means of realizing the kototama, yet the magical power of sound has been a medium of spiritual practice since the dawn of human civilization for, among others, "the Rishis who inhabited the slopes of the Himalayas, the Magi of Iran, the adepts of Mesopotamia, the priests of Egypt, and the mystics of Greece—to mention only those of whom tradition has left some traces."[4]

The Biblical logos, "In the beginning was the word," was passed down in India as early as 400 BCE. In the Vedas, the holy book of India, we find this same teaching: "In the beginning was Brahman with whom was the word, and the word is Brahman (God)." The origins of Christianity are a great deal older than is commonly assumed. The original teachings of the human race on this planet are long since lost in the division between human history and mythology.

Jesus Christ was a member of the Essenes. "The Essene people, spread out along the river of Jordan, were studying a synthesis of Greek philosophy, especially Pythagorean thought, traditional Judaism, and, according to many opinions, the philosophy and cosmology of the East. . . . These people were called 'followers of the way of Krishna,' a legendary figure in India. The name 'Christian' may have developed as a result of this."[5]

The Assyrian church is the original Christian church in what is today eastern Iraq and Iran. The Assyrian church, also referred to as the Nestorian church, reached India at an early date and traveled to China and Mongolia in the early seventh century. The Nestorians taught that Christ exists as the man, Jesus, and also as the divine son of God, or logos.

This teaching of logos, or the word as God, spread to China and Japan as Keikyo, the name of which translates as "the divine shining light." In Buddhism it was also passed down in the Shingon Mikkyo sect as the practice of *ajikan,* meditation on the sacred syllable of A. Shingon Mikkyo means "the secret teaching of the true word." The name of the Buddhist deity Kannon contains the meaning of *seeing sound with the mind's eye.*

In the words of the Tibetan guru Lama Govinda,

The idea of creative sound was continued in the teachings of logos, which were partly absorbed by early Christianity, as we can see from the Gospel of St. John, which begins with the mysterious words: [In the beginning was the word, and the word was with God, and the word was God . . . and the word was made flesh . . .].

If these profound teachings, which were about to link up Christianity with Gnostic philosophy and the traditions of the East, had been able to maintain their influence, the universal message of Christ would have been saved from the pitfalls of intolerance and narrow-mindedness.[6]

In the words of kototama scholar Koji Ogasawara,

Buddha teaches that the *mani* jewel (kototama) is compulsory study for a Bodhisattva to become a Buddha. This lies two steps deeper than the basic enlightenment of religion. To understand pure kototama you must get rid of the old karmic crust and skin and become like an innocent baby. This is called *resurrection* in Christianity, and *enlightenment* in Buddhism.

Therefore you first must graduate from the mind of ancient religion by being obedient pupils of the ancient sages. . . . To graduate from these religions does not mean to ignore them or disregard them, but to understand them with body and soul.[7]

O-sensei's practice of Aikido was at one with this attitude. He rose early every morning for the chanting of Shinto prayers, and he was a diligent student of the ancient spiritual texts. In his studies with Deguchi Onisaburo he also practiced deep meditation, sometimes lasting through the night. His level of intuitive development was a result of this attitude as much as it was of his daily training in Aikido.

In modern Japanese Shinto, which is clothed in religious overtones, the kototama is symbolized as *shinreikai,* the realm of the gods. It is the storehouse consciousness, the seventh and eighth levels of spirit, which can be clearly perceived only by the enlightened mind.

神霊界

■ *Shinreikai*

Shinreikai is the world of *sonen,* consciousness at a level deeper than the subconscious mind.

Although both our thoughts and our feelings originate in sonen, we can't access this aspect of mind through abstract thought. It is only when our feelings and actions come from a place of intense sincerity and honesty (*makoto*) that the world of sonen is influenced. If we deeply feel goodness and express it with our words and actions, good things will be brought forth. This is a fundamental truth of the kototama.

The original practice of Shinto, as well as that of Tibetan mysticism, approaches this awakening through meditation on certain deities, chanting, and *misogi,* or purification rituals. In some cases these are combined, such as chanting beneath waterfalls or meditating for long periods without food or sleep. The purpose of this misogi is to clear the mind of thought and align our ki with the kototama.

The study of Aikido is at one with the teachings of the ancient sages. With the creation of Aikido, however, O-sensei removed the veil surrounding the various religious expressions and made misogi more readily accessible. Through his daily *shugyo,* or spiritual training, he was able to experience deep spiritual transformation. *When I chant the sounds of the various kototama, the deities associated with those sounds gather around me.*

The founder stated, *If your mind deviates from that of the great creator spirit of the universe, you aren't really doing Aikido.* Not only our actions but also our thoughts and feelings activate universal ki and bring about the events that shape our lives. This is the reality of the kototama, or word *spirit.* Understanding this, O-sensei's vision was one of healing ourselves and our planet through our own spiritual training.

The kototama of I and Su are the beginning from which all else springs forth. Perhaps it is for this reason that the main shrine in Japan is named Ise Jingu, and the river that flows through it is called Isuzu, the River of Fifty Bells, indicating the sounds of the kototama. In order to manifest itself Su gives birth to the four dimensions of ki. From a spiritual point of view, these are called the four souls.

■ *Sonen*

Aikitama: The Spirit of
Universal Harmony

■ *Ichirei shikon*

一霊四魂

ICHIREI SHIKON: ONE SPIRIT, FOUR SOULS

The subject of one spirit and four souls is covered in considerable depth in *The Spiritual Foundations of Aikido,* so it will be somewhat abbreviated here. In the original teachings of Shinto, mankind was assumed to be a descendant of the gods. This was perhaps the foundation of ancestor worship as it continues today. It was taught that the human race was of only one origin, yet there were five different auras, or spiritual orientations.

The Takeuchi Documents record the earliest ancestors of the human race as *go shiki jin,* the five different-colored races. Actually there was only one race, yet people were distinguished by the color of their spiritual aura. The yellow people were the lineage of the sun-worshipping race (I). Their spiritual aura was dominated by the influence of Kushitama.

The Hebrew people were the red people, the ancestors of Akahitomeso (E). This is the soul of Aratama. There were also the purple people (O–Nigitama), the white people (U–Naohi), and the blue people (A–Sakitama). These are still worshipped in a few ancient shrines in Japan as the original ancestors of humankind. Five very old masks carved in wood were discovered at a shrine in southern Japan as the main objects of worship.

The deities represented by these five masks are called the ancient ancestors of humankind, yet they are not our human ancestors; they represent the dimensions of universal spirit. The universal spirit, in turn, is divided into four souls. This universal deity (Ame no Minaka Nushi) is divided into three aspects: spirit, power, and body.

Spirit, in this explanation, refers to one spirit and four souls. Power refers to the eight powers, the rhythms of movement. Body, in Shinto, is understood as the function of the spirit.

Body, the physical world, is sometimes called *utsushiyo,* "the reflected world." This means that the world we perceive is a reflection

of our own mind. In other words, it is the world divided into subject and object, physical and spiritual, and so forth. Until we return to the absolute perspective of here and now, we cannot grasp this world as a product of our own mind.

Naohi: The Spirit of Self-Reflection

The universal body, when seen as our personal spirit, is called *naohi*, the kototama of Su and U. The four dimensions through which it is expressed are Aratama (E), Kushitama (I), Nigitama (O), and Sakitama (A). Like a cup of water taken from the ocean, the spirit of human beings and that of the universe with its boundless scope are exactly the same. Naohi, our direct spirit, is the mirror mind of perfect wisdom, the quality of clear reflection. It is this function that makes possible the awakening of human potential.

Just as our physical organs exist fundamentally for the purpose of biological transmutation, and thereby for the continuation of our life,

■ *Naohi*

Aikitama: The Spirit of Universal Harmony

21

so the soul and spirit exist fundamentally as a means for self-reflection in order to maintain health of mind and feeling. Each of the four souls presides over a different aspect of our psychological and spiritual makeup.

It is almost impossible for the ability of self-reflection to be totally lost. If this were to occur, we would lose all semblance of human quality and degenerate into something far more frightening than any of the beasts of the earth. There would be no means by which to correct the downward spiral of degeneration. When self-reflection and sincerity, the direct attributes of naohi, are strengthened, however, so are the virtues of each of the four souls.

Kushitama: The Mysterious Soul

■ *Kushitama*

Kushitama is called "the mysterious soul." It is based on the kototama of I, which creates pure perception and intuition. Like salt in the ocean, Kushitama remains hidden at the center of existence. As it is the source of perception itself, this is the most difficult aspect of our soul and spirit to perceive. It is the power of centeredness, self-control, and spiritual enlightenment.

Kushitama gives us sensitivity, and therefore the potential of perfect wisdom. It is the ability to immediately and correctly respond to the imperative of any situation. The sensitive nature of Kushitama must be clothed in the peacefulness of the five senses. If our senses are excited, clear perception is lost.

The incredible sharpness of I therefore remains hidden deep within the water ki of Su. From this place it becomes the motive power by which all movement and reality are born. In the words of O-sensei, *Kushitama is principle, the divine authority (miizu) of Heaven. It is the complete manifestation of the virtue of the creator spirit of Su.*

Converting the ignorance of a dualistic perspective into the wisdom of unity—this is the function of Kushitama. If this quality is maintained, Kushitama becomes our antennae for perceiving the subtlest vibrations of reality. It provides us with the greatest beauty of the human soul. If, however, our senses run wild and we encounter excessive stress, the sensitive function of Kushitama can be damaged. This is very dangerous. In extreme cases, it can become true insanity.

Aratama: The Soul of Refinement

Aratama is fire ki, the kototama of E dimension. Literally it means "rough soul," yet it is also the power of refinement. Its symbol is the sword, which can be a rough weapon of destruction or an elegant tool of refinement. Aratama is the sword of human judgment—that which is used to cut through delusion and toward clarity and precision.

■ *Aratama*

In Zen Buddhism it is called "the way to cross the river when the bridge is down." In the Bible it is Aaron's rod and, again, the staff Moses used to part the waters. Human judgment is the only thing man can really depend upon, the only tool with which to grasp *michi,* or the way of life.

Once again, here are the words of Morihei Ueshiba:

> *Aratama is Ho (law, method, dharma). It is that which must be done. It means to solve the mystery of universal principle and thereby to securely hold the virtues of the four souls within your hara. To do so is to master the way of Heaven and pass it down to others. In other words, it is to unite (*matsuri*) Heaven and Earth.*

Aratama is also the soul of courage. It is the power to seek truth, and thereby to release us from attachment, allowing us to leap beyond the self-imposed restrictions that hinder our spiritual growth. If we don't use our E dimension capability to refine our rough soul, we human beings remain quite similar to an angry bull in a china shop. This is truly unsightly. Elegance and grace cannot survive even for a moment in an environment of anger.

As we refine our method of doing things, we no longer meet opposition head-on, and anger gradually disappears from our countenance. Using our judgment to discern the most economic and expedient way of living our life, we also gain a sense of orderliness. This is the interchange between Aratama and Nigitama.

Nigitama: The Soul of Nurturing

Nigitama is water ki, the kototama of O dimension. Its symbol is the mani jewel, or beads, which in turn represent the word souls, or kototama. Nigitama is the power of tying things together for their

■ *Nigitama*

continuation. It ties the word souls together as memory and consciousness, making human progress possible.

Nigitama seeks love and warmth—the feeling in which all things are seen as timeless and perfect. If the feeling of love is lost, Nigitama is dead. Like water in winter, it becomes frozen, rigid, and hateful. Through the power of memory, however, we are able to reflect on the past and amend our mistaken attitudes and feelings.

It is this ability that maintains Nigitama in a healthy state. O-sensei referred to this soul as the quality of *banyu aigo,* caring for and nurturing human society and all of life. This is the ki of spiritual maturity and greatness. It is compassion manifest in daily life. In the words of O-sensei:

> *Nigitama is water ki. It is the mutual exchange of love, which comes forth as the quality of firm yet peaceful leadership. Lacking complete sincerity, it cannot succeed. Acting with propriety and proper decor (*rei*), it works to establish harmony between all people, regardless of their position in life.*

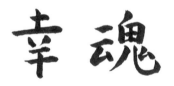

■ *Sakitama*

Sakitama: The Soul of Abundance

Sakitama is called the soul of happiness and success, yet this is a superficial explanation. Sakitama is the kototama of A, the origin and continual support of awareness. It is the ki of spiritual abundance that creates the material world. It is the soul of youth and aspiration, of positive thought and dreams of greatness.

O-sensei sometimes referred to it as Kuni toko tachi no kami, the deity that establishes the material world. *When Kuni toko tachi no kami (A) interacts with Toyo kumo no kami (O), the five deities of manifestation begin their function.* Here the founder is referring to A and O dimensions' ki as the interchange of centripetal and centrifugal force.

The way of earth is michi; it is to manifest the divine authority of Kushitama on this earth. Michi means holding the truth of ultimate reality in your own hara as closely as the blood that circulates in your body.

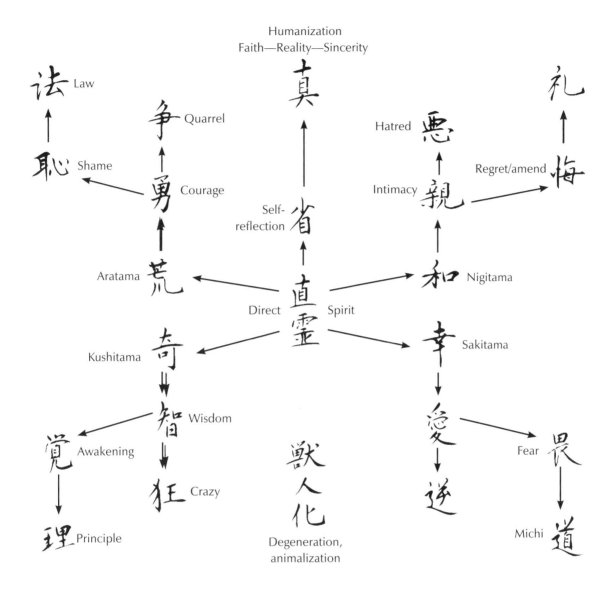

■ *Fig. 1.7. Ichirei, shikon: one spirit, four souls*

The spiritual light of A dimension's ki is often felt to be our true nature, yet this leads toward egocentric thinking. This way of thinking is common in religious circles and leads to a kind of yang arrogance, a feeling of superiority over others. In order to counter this feeling, A dimension also creates a sense of awe and wonder at the mysteries of life.

In Christianity this is called the "fear of God," yet fear of any kind is never a virtue. Rather it should be understood as appreciation,

Aikitama: The Spirit of Universal Harmony

or gratitude. The balance between gratitude and a positive sense of one's own ability helps us maintain beginner's mind and a sense of humility.

The study of Aikido, like all spiritual disciplines, develops certain powers, abilities, and charisma. If we lack humility, these very benefits can become obstructions. This is especially true for those who would become teachers. The teacher's mission is to help the students become strong, healthy, and free individuals. It is the teacher, even more than the student, who receives the greatest benefit from this mutually beneficial relationship.

Without the student, there can be no teacher. The teacher who seeks to have his students serve him or stroke his ego creates slaves and eventually will fail. It is important to neither ignore nor rigidly follow form and protocol. The heart is more important than outward appearance or form. "Etiquette is not needed in an environment where people are real."[8]

As the light of mind, Sakitama is the beginning of michi, the road to clarity and higher judgment. Sakitama is the source of spiritual feeling, and when it is healthy we naturally gravitate toward the infinite mystery of life; yet our feet remain firmly planted on the ground of michi, the path toward realization.

CLASSIFICATION OF THE VOWEL DIMENSIONS

The religious expression "one spirit, four souls" refers to the five dimensions of nature and the universe. In Shinto these dimensions of ki are referred to as Hitori gami, which means "individual deity." Hitori gami is an entity that occupies the whole universe by itself and is omnipresent in it. That universe is called a dimension.[9]

In the moment of expansion there is only expansion. In the moment of simple being there is nothing but being. This is not objective reality; it is subjective, one-pointed perception existing only here and now. It is considered as "layered" dimensions that never meet.

Just as white clouds do not obscure the blue sky, I dimension's ki becomes established as the absolute center within the space of U dimension's ki. This becomes the stabilizing force of gravity that holds life ki at the center of our hara. It is the kototama of Wi, the wellspring of life ki. In the endless time-space continuum of relativity, all five dimensions are mutually arising and totally interdependent.

Our perception begins with awareness and feeling. This is called *ana,* or the vibration of Heaven. When the five dimensions are united and stabilized by the eight powers of I dimension, the idea, or intention, of creation begins. This is *mana,* the realm of thought from which all manifestation is born. Let us consider the basic function of each dimension and how they relate to one another.

The classification of the five vowel dimensions is at the basis of practically every major religious and philosophical tradition that has survived to the present day. In Buddhism they represent the five vehicles, or *sattvas.* U dimension is *sattva-yana*, the body, or vehicle, itself. Merely by being born as a human being, however unrealized, you are automatically in the class of sattva.

O dimension is *sravaka-yana.* This is usually considered the first stage. It is the level at which we have considered the teachings and thus rid ourselves of dogma and the idea of the permanency of phenomenon. The progression of nature is AOEI, yet it seems that human beings, with their ability to think in the abstract, sometimes must proceed with the conceptual mind first.

A dimension is *pratyeka-yana.* In Buddhism it is referred to as the second stage, the *hinayana,* or small vehicle. This is one who is satisfied with dwelling in the realm of the five dimensions yet cannot manifest it in society for the sake of others. As we will see in chapter 5, the Shinto view of development proceeds in the order of nature mentioned above.

E dimension is the Boddhisattva-yana. The Boddhisattva trains himself solely for the sake of others. This is the realm of Mahayana Buddhism. This mentality is said to be beyond the conception of ordinary people. It is called "the gate of awakening," the realm of subtle differentiation.

I dimension is the Buddha vehicle, which unites all the rest. It is *nakaima,* the absolute here and now. It is called the "gate of nirvana," or the realm of ultimate wisdom. There is no longer any dependency on training, yet training continues without one's even being aware of it.

When the spark of intention flies between subjective mind and objective reality, the truth of reality is revealed. It is said that this is the only thing the Buddha keeps in mind. Coming from the absolute freedom of I dimension, one may freely wield the sword of judgment depending on the criterion of the moment. Wielding the sword of judgment from this place manifests the kototama of IE.

In the classical Chinese tradition, the dimensions were classified by the legendary emperor Fsu Hi as large yin (A), large yang (O), small yin (E), small yang (I), and the absolute, or *taikyoku* (U). The Yellow Emperor further subdivided these into earth (U), water (O), fire (I), metal (E), and wood (A). In this way of seeing, U dimension is placed in the center.

I

A   U   E

O

■ *Fig. 1.8. Vowels with U at the center*

The main confusion arises in regard to the element of earth. It can mean the planet Earth, the mineral content of the soil, and even the ground of being. This will be addressed below, but first it is important not to literally equate the terms *yin* and *yang* with the elements of fire and water.

In the Chinese classics, fire is seen as yin and water is understood as yang. This view sees fire and water as aspects of consciousness, rather than as physical elements. The ki of fire is fleeting and gives us spiritual insight, while the ki of water is the power of materialization and supports the continuation of the physical world.

This also may be understood in a physical sense, if we see that the minority always rules over the majority. Fire is two parts yang on the surface, yet the center is yin. We see this in the I Ching, the Chinese classic of divination, which places one broken (yin) line between two solid (yang) lines to represent the element of fire. The trigram for water is just the opposite.

When the five elements are seen as the dimensions of universal ki, they are understood to be the most fundamental aspects of our consciousness. The order in which they develop, therefore, changes our perspective on reality. The kototama principle divides these dimensions into three different orders, each representing a different worldview, or approach to life.

Kanagi, the first order, develops a strictly materialistic interpretation of reality. Kanagi deals with the matter (*gi*) of form (*kana*). In other words, it deals with visible and obvious form and doesn't concern itself with hidden or invisible reality. Following the kanagi order, one develops in the pattern of UEO—consciousness based on the five senses, the realm of U dimension.

In this order we see the world from the view of the five senses (U), and our judgment (E) serves to fulfill the desires arising from that perspective. This, in turn, is remembered and repeated due to the function of our memory (O). The process repeats itself endlessly and thereby imprisons the mind.

The *sugaso* order is AOUE. The spiritual feeling of A dimension is given continuity by O. This, in turn, is manifest through the senses (U) and judged by our E dimension's capacity. This order creates a view of life based on a more abstract or philosophical way of thinking, yet in the end it is also materialistic and dualistic and cannot, therefore, reach complete understanding.

Sugaso gives birth to the various religious interpretations of truth and reality, yet being based on an infinitely expanding and ultimately unreachable absolute, it is forced to return on itself and find salvation in materialistic ideas of a paradise after death. The perspective of U and that of A are irreconcilably opposed to each other. Nevertheless, each has its value and is an essential ingredient in our growth and understanding.

The kanagi order was used by O-sensei's spiritual teacher, Deguchi Onisaburo, to classify the vowel dimensions, yet he used the sugaso order when discussing spiritual development. Ueshiba O-sensei also used these two systems at different times in order to show physical or spiritual aspects of Aikido.

In the *Dai Nippon Shinten,* a text used in the education of the Japanese emperor, the order of sugaso is expressed as follows:

Opening the mouth wide and pushing breath outward from the depths of your throat, the sound of A continues unchanged regardless of how long you continue. This is called Kuni toko tachi no kami, the god that continually established the material world. This void is received by Izanagi no kami (I) and Izanami no kami (Wi).

Gradually closing the mouth until the lips make the shape of a round cloud (*kumo*), the breath catches in the throat (*toyo*) and the sound of O comes forth naturally. It is therefore called Toyokumo no kami. Further closing the lips, the sound of U comes forth. This is called Uhijini no kami. As we push the voice of U out strongly, it naturally returns to Su. This is called Suhijini no kami.

From the sound of U, thrust the tongue forward against the lower jaw like a stake (*kui*) and the sound of E comes forth. This is called Tsunugui no kami and is said to accompany the opening of spiritual vision. Voicing the sound of E with power, the tip of the tongue shifts upward reaching the upper jaw and produces the sound of Re. This is called Ikugui no kami.

Continuing to make the sound of Re, the breath cycles upward creating the vibration of Re-I. Forcefully making the sound of I, it reaches its extreme in the sound of Gi. This is the great end of the voice and is likened to the deities of Ohotonoji no kami and Ohotonobe no kami.[10]

Ueshiba O-sensei quoted from the *Kototama Hissho* of Yamaguchi Shido such phrases as *In stillness, water ki is horizontal and fire ki is vertical. In motion, water ki stands up and fire ki branches outward.* This refers to the kototama of E and I from the kanagi view, within which I is fire ki and E is water ki. Again from the Japanese Kojiki, the book of ancient events, the founder quoted the teaching, *In the beginning the lighter, more ethereal ki (the kototama of A) rose upward, creating the heavens, while the heavier, coarser ki (the kototama of O) sank down to create the earth.* This is based on the same kanagi view.

Following the teachings of *Dai Nippon Shinten,* the founder referred to earth ki as Kuni toko tachi no kami, the kototama of A.

Nevertheless, when demonstrating the beautiful and flowing movements of Aikido, O-sensei was known to chant the sugaso order of AOUEI. In other words, it was not uncommon for teachers at that time to use the system most suited to the aspect they were emphasizing. The kanagi order:

A - Heaven
I - Fire
U - Unity
E - Water
O - Earth

The sugaso order:

> A - Heaven
> O - Water
> U - Unity
> E - Fire
> I - Earth

In contrast to the objective teachings of kanagi and sugaso above, the *Dai Nippon Shinten* approaches the elements from a completely subjective point of view. Heaven is seen as I dimension because it is the source of our most sensitive perception and spiritual intuition. Earth, on the other hand, is seen as A dimension because as the source of conscious awareness, it lights up—and thereby manifests—the world of phenomenon.

> Kushitama (I-Gi) expresses the greatest wealth of both Heaven and Earth, and our individual spirit as well. It is therefore symbolized by Heaven. Aratama (E-Re) gives warmth and heat to the universe, and thus is represented by fire. Nigitama (O) is flexible and unites all the opposing factors of society and the world. It provides for flexibility within structure, and thus is represented by water. Sakitama (A) brings forth stark reality and the formation or consolidation of the world. Therefore, it is represented by earth.[11]

Above we have both the objective and the subjective interpretation of the five dimensions, yet there is no unity. In order to see the larger, more all-encompassing view of body and spirit as one, we need to study the *amatsu futonorito* order. This merges perfectly with the Chinese idea of *ten-jin-chi,* or human beings standing between and unifying Heaven and Earth.

The futonorito order is based on the kototama of IE. Traditionally it is seen as the order of AIEOU, yet it can also be understood as AEIOU. Because the perfect wisdom of I dimension can be reached only through the development of E dimension, I may be placed both before and after E dimension. When I dimension is realized, however, it automatically manifests itself as the perfect judgment of IE.

The futonorito order is the expression of *futomani,* the perfected order of consciousness. Omitting the rows of A and Wa, it divides the fifty pure sounds of the kototama into twenty sounds of Heaven and twenty sounds of Earth. This is the boat (*fune*) necessary for crossing over to *higan,* the other shore, or enlightenment.

The futonorito order:

A - Heaven
E - Fire
I - Human being
O - Water
U - Earth

The name of each of the three orders is preceded by the word *amatsu,* which means "that which is contained within Heaven." *Futo* is the number twenty, half of the word souls minus the rows of Heaven (A) and Earth (Wa). When the ten rows are combined, they represent the perfection of Heaven on Earth. *Norito* means "prayer." The meaning of *futonorito,* therefore, is similar to that found in the Lord's Prayer, "Thy will be done, on Earth as it is in Heaven."

These three orders of the kototama will be discussed in greater detail in chapters 4 and 5. Let it suffice here to explain that the futonorito order is the most immediately applicable to both Aikido principle and movement and will be used here in discussing both spiritual and physical aspects of Aikido training, unless otherwise specified.

Within the various sects of both Shinto and Buddhism, the classification of elements is not consistent; it changes with the view being expressed and sometimes depends on the physical experience of the practitioner. The vowel dimensions, however, although they have many aspects, are unchanging. For our practice it is important to understand how they relate to each other both physically and spiritually.

"The starting point of the Buddhist yoga is of neither cosmological nor theo-metaphysical character, but physiological in the deepest sense. Thus the character of the psychic centers is not determined by the qualities of the elements, but by the psychological functions which are ascribed or consciously attributed to them."[12]

U Dimension: Spirit and Body as One—The Ki of Earth

In discussing the kototama of Su, many of the sounds of U dimension were introduced. U dimension is the world as perceived by our five senses. It is gross matter and also the ki that fills the hollow shell that we call our body. It is the body moving through ki, and ki moving through the body.

In the Shinto view, the body of the universe is spirit, or ki, and the visible, or reflected world, is the function of that ki. The realm of ki creates the relative world of vibration. Vibration, in turn, is transformed into the state of preatomic elements. This fragile fire ki of the ionosphere, further materialized by the centripetal force of O dimension's ki, manifests the physical elements that compose matter and life.

It is much like the process of water freezing in the winter. As it becomes solid it expands outward, leaving the inside empty. In the same way, our physical body and all physical matter are frozen at this temperature. In other words, matter is basically empty. This emptiness is U dimension—the great unity, or *musubi,* of matter and spiritual ki.

U dimension's consciousness is mechanical. It is limited to the direct perception of the five senses, yet there is no ability of recognition, or distinction of one thing from another. In Buddhism it is called *geza,* the lower world, or hell. This means that there is, as of yet, no ability of word consciousness; the mind is trapped and unable to express itself.

Mussels on a rock by the sea are an ancient form of life. They have no eye, ear, nose, or tongue. Although they have a mind, it is nothing other than their body. Their mind is their skin, and the only sense they rely upon is the sense of touch. This seems incredibly basic, yet their sense of touch borders on what human beings would call telepathic.

If you place your hand above a mussel, it senses your presence and immediately retreats within its shell. A mussel's sense of touch relies solely on its ki. In the same way all of our senses actually depend first on the sense of touch, the electrical impulses that make perception possible to the brain.

The original brain is the membrane of the cell, not the nucleus as was formerly believed. Just as in the first cell of life, our skin and sense of touch is our most fundamental communication with the environment. If this sensitivity is lost, we lose the foundation of our highest spiritual sensitivity. Without this sensitivity, our intuition, based on I dimension, cannot develop. Realistic spiritual development, therefore, begins with training the body.

It is only through the body that we can discover the spirit. The Japanese word for body is *karada*. *Kara* means "empty," and Ta is the energy field of hara, the ki that supports life. As expressed in the Heart Sutra of Buddhism, "Emptiness is exactly form; form is exactly emptiness."

In our practice we should come to feel the emptiness of our physical body. When all tension is gone and our ki is constantly expanding, our body is realized as an empty vessel of ki. The physical body is extremely fragile. Muscles are easily injured and bones easily broken. Our ki, however, when it is strongly focused, can be more durable and longer lasting and can produce much greater power.

The source of our spirit, or ki, is the very emptiness of our body. In Mahayana Buddhism, U dimension is the great body of the universe, the Dharmakaya Vairocana. This is the ground of being, or original consciousness. U dimension is hara, the source of both body and mind. For the practice of Aikido, it should be understood as earth ki.

A Dimension: The Expansive Ki of Heaven

The fundamental quality of A dimension is *hiraki,* or expansion. As infinite expansion, it is the ki that gives birth to all things. Infinite expansion (A) meeting itself (Wa) sees it as other. For this reason there is relative movement within the absolute. A dimension begins as the ability of sensory judgment and feeling, yet at it highest development it brings forth the qualities of mercy and compassion.

As the expansion of awareness it should be classified as Heaven. A is called the "firstborn." It is the light of consciousness, that which reveals the relative world as subject and object, self and other. In Genesis it is the dividing of Heaven from Earth, that which occurred following our awakening to consciousness when God said, "Let there be light."[13]

In the ancient teachings of the East, the world was created not only by our heavenly father, but also by our earthly mother. This is a reference to the kototama of A and O, centrifugal and centripetal force. A dimension creates our spiritual capacity, and O dimension creates our memory and the ability to manifest ideas as reality.

The kototama of A supports all movement and existence. If we lose the lightness of A dimension's expanding ki, we lose our life force. If the ki of A dimension becomes weak in our body, the feeling of youthfulness disappears and our life force begins to wither and die. In Aikido it is the life of the technique. If it is lost we must return to reliance on physical force and manipulation.

A is the ruler of the vowel dimensions, which, as a unit, are classified as *water ki within the empty sky, the ki of U dimension*. The vowels AIEOU are subjective mind, as contrasted with the objectivity of Wa Wi We Wo Wu. Seen in this way, the vowels as a unit are the ki of Heaven, and the semi-vowels, beginning with the sound of U, are the ki of Earth. Standing between and unifying these two is Ya Yi Ye Yo Yu, the kototama that creates our most important human uniqueness, the ability of self-realization.

A dimension's infinite expansion never returns or implodes upon itself. This must be grasped in your feeling as you practice. It should be understood not only as the rising ki of the upper body, but also as expansion in all directions from your one point. Within the continually expanding feeling of A, the relative expansion (E) and contraction (O) of the technique alternates.

In Aikido practice, expansion is the first movement of your body and should accompany your *de-ai,* or coming out to meet your partner's attack. The de-ai is for the purpose of receiving and drawing your partner's ki into your center. When your feeling is expanding outward (A) and your natural weight (O) is resting on your partner's body, his ki automatically rises upward and weakens his balance.

If this expansion is given proper direction through the function of

E dimension's ki, you will keep your partner off balance with a minimum of effort. There should be no clamping down, or killing the ki of the technique. You should bring the vowel dimensions into your practice by studying the way of holding your body, the way of touch, and the direction and unification of your ki. Every aspect of your feeling derives from the ki of the vowel dimensions.

O Dimension: The Connecting Ki of Water

As A is the dimension of expansion, O is contraction, continuation, and materialization. It is *matomari,* or bringing things together in unity and coherence. This should not be mistaken for the power of tightening around your partner's body. It is more like holding a small child, carefully encompassing, yet with gentleness. When A is compared with O, they may be seen as Heaven and Earth. When E and O work together, however, they should be understood as fire and water.

Like water, flexibly seeking the lowest resting place, weight and concentration create power. The total flexibility of water makes it appear yin, or passive, yet at its center it is yang, the source of our physical power. O dimension is the power of *omoi,* which means both "weight" and "thought." It is the concentration of ki, which connects our body and mind with that of our partner. As the power of concentration, it also produces continuance. The word *ki-musubi,* in Aikido, describes the fully connected situation in which we harmonize with our partner's movement yet maintain whole body unification.

O dimension is also described as *osameru,* "to control" or "to bring things to a conclusion." The statement of the founder, *Bring your partner down in the sign of the square,* is using O dimension in this way. Again, this should not be mistaken for pushing down on your partner or applying pressure from above. Leading your partner outward horizontally with E dimension's ki is what keeps him off balance.

To manifest O dimension properly, your natural weight rides on your partner's center and is given direction through your fingertips— the ki of E dimension. It is like a leaf falling from a tree in the autumn. It glides from left to right as it descends toward the ground, or it spirals downward. Both of these show the ki of E dimension.

E Dimension: The Cycling Ki of Fire

E dimension is called *kaiten,* or cycling, yet once again this is much too vague. It is the fire ki of E dimension that gives direction to the infinitely expanding ki of Heaven (A). Branching outward from pure expansion, the movement of fire ki begins to cycle and create form.

E dimension is the power of judgment, the beginning of distinctly human mentality. It gives direction to mind and thereby creates movement and form. It gives us the ability of abstract thought, to consciously create an image in our mind. O-sensei called it *masakatsu,* or the correct way of accomplishing things.

Fire (E) and water (O) are the servants of Heaven and Earth, the active elements in movement. In our psychological constitution they are the constant interchange between judgment and memory. Our depth of wisdom, our realization of I dimension, determines how well these are balanced.

All things are determined by the balance of fire and water ki. If they are well balanced, life leads us toward health, clarity, harmony, and wisdom. Fire ki must always lead our direction, both physically and mentally. The ki of water creates continuance and power, yet without direction power is worthless.

In Aikido practice, the direction of your fingers creates the form of the technique. Your fingers show your judgment, the direction of your mind and ki. The power of fire ki is tenacity; like fire on wood, it adheres without grasping. As you open your hands and breathe inward, you hold your partner with your mind. As long as your fingers can move freely, your mind is free and your movement cannot be restrained.

If you are truly free from feelings of competition and self-protection, your mind will automatically seek out the path of least resistance, and your fingers will express a direction toward freedom. When this happens, your partner's efforts to restrict your movement will be in vain.

I Dimension: The Ki of Volition

The dimension of I has so many important implications, yet in a word it is described as *hataraki,* or the motive power of life. It is the life will and power. It always remains hidden, yet once it is realized, it actually becomes the subtle function of Aikido technique. It is from one point, the kototama of I, that the ki of fire and water perform their functions. When considered in this way, I dimension should be seen as the ki of earth. As the reality of Kushitama, the mysterious soul, I dimension is able to change its nature depending on the circumstances.

In stillness it may be seen as water ki, yet when activated, it comes forth as the ki of fire. When seen as tanden no ichi, the stabilizing influence of one point, it is earth ki. As the origin of function, it is called by different names including *hochi, kori, chi,* and Si. It is the unborn seed of life within the womb of Su.

As our spiritual antennae, it creates our most subtle and sensitive perception. For this reason, it is also the most difficult part of our nature to realize. Fully grasped, it creates an unshakeable faith in here and now, in existence itself. This kind of faith is the ultimate goal, and also the mastery of Aikido. When it is grasped, our posture becomes naturally upright and all tension is gone from both body and mind.

When we grasp I dimension as the origin and control point of our own existence, attachment no longer makes any sense. When we attempt to take hold of this essence, it disappears immediately. In order to experience the quality of I dimension, we must be very sensitive receivers. The quality of our life is largely determined by the way we see it, yet mankind is forever the *uke* (receiver) of life, never its creator.

I dimension has no physical counterpart we can feel or to which we can relate. It is the meeting point of the ki of Heaven and Earth, and our power is the result of receiving this ki in our hara and giving it a new direction through E dimension's ki. It is that which transforms our physical center into our psychic center. When our attention is focused in our one point, we are able to initiate subtle changes in our body's ki with one movement of our mind.

In Aikido practice, one point, and the vertical ki that rises up from it, is like the center post of an umbrella, unifying all directions under one center. When we see only the two sides of any equation, we are unbalanced. There is a third aspect, unperceivable to the five senses. To see it is to open your spiritual eyes.

This was expressed by O-sensei as *katsu hayabi,* which may be translated as "an immediate and perfect response." When our mind is firmly focused in our one point, our movement is spontaneous and immediate. This is the quality of the enlightened mind. A perfect response requires perfect perception, perfect receiving.

This kind of feeling requires great faith in all things—in life itself. It requires raising our level of perception to clearly see beyond the illusion of separateness and duality. As our experience is retained and evaluated in the moment, our judgment passes, step by step, through the eight powers. Finally we reach the place where creativity is spontaneous and without hindrance, coming from the eight powers of I dimension.

Hachi Riki: The Eight Powers

As described above, I and Wi, the life will and power, are the creative volition of life. To paraphrase from the teachings of kototama scholar Koji Ogasawara, *To momentarily and inwardly experience the moment when the spiritual wave of mind sparks between subject and object—this is recognition of actual reality.* It is one of the main goals of Zen practice. A priori, being universal, this experience of reality is also universal. Standing at the fulcrum of nakaima, the absolute here and now, traceless enightenment unfolds from moment to moment.

The sparks of real perception appear as the eight vibrations of Hi Ti Si Ki Mi Ri Yi Ni. They are also called *ame no uki hashi,* or the floating bridge of Heaven. It is the bridge that connects consciousness and phenomenon. In Buddhism it is the bridge that one must cross to reach the other shore, or enlightened mind.

The root of subjective consciousness (AIUEO) is the voice of A. The root of objective consciousness (Wa Wi Wu We Wo) is the voice of U. In the words of O-sensei,

> *Ame no uki hashi is the bridge connecting Heaven (AOUEI) and Earth (Wa Wo Wu We Wi) and all opposing forces. A and U become O. When this kototama is manifest in the world it is the sacred syllable of AUM or Om. Standing on ame no uki hashi is to stand between and unify all opposing forces; it is to embody the divine authority* (miizu) *of Ame no Minaka Nushi, the kototama of Su.*

To stand on ame no uki hashi is to be coming from I dimension and to express it as Ya Yi Ye Yo Yu. It is to be rooted in nakaima, the absolute here and now. The preparation for this ability occurs in stages, gradually leading to the subtlety of the enlightened mind.

The process of creation in nature and the process of human development follow the same pattern. Each takes place in seven levels before disappearing once more into the realm of Hi, or pure spirit, from which it began. These stages are shown in the colors of the rainbow, in the eight moral principles of Buddhism, and also in the eightfold path of Ama terasu oh mikami, the Sun goddess (see page 216).

The creation of the universe begins from moment to moment with one thought. In Buddhism it is called *ichinen,* the momentary spark of perception that occurs within nakaima. This is simple being and receiving, as opposed to movement or doing. I dimension therefore stands aside from the other vowels as the vehicle of the eight powers.

The manifest world is based on spiral form, yet it is *iki,* the straight lines of I dimension's ki, that give it life, stability, and actual substance. When iki, life will, and power are firmly rooted in your hara, the real meaning of *shin,* or faith, is realized, and judgment becomes clear and precise.

In contrast to the vowel dimensions, or "mother sounds," the eight powers are referred to as "father rhythms." As these vibrations reach higher frequency, the intensity of our ki increases and our perception becomes more accurate and precise. As our ki becomes more intense, our body should become more relaxed and at peace. In this way our physical, psychological, and spiritual growth gradually unfolds.

This process begins, first of all, in the realm of feeling or spirit. It is described as *amatsu iwasaka,* or the five levels of Heaven's ki. In the Shinto explanation of creation, the five levels of amatsu iwasaka are composed of seventeen deities.

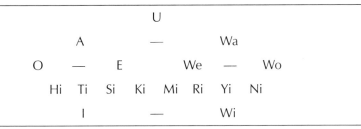

			U				
	A		—		Wa		
O	—	E		We	—	Wo	
Hi	Ti	Si	Ki	Mi	Ri	Yi	Ni
	I		—		Wi		

■ *Fig. 1.9. The seventeen sounds of amatsu iwasaka*

Each of the seventeen deities of amatsu iwasaka serves a particular function in the creation of form, movement, and consciousness. For our purposes here, I will mention the names of only the first three. They are Ame no Minaka Nushi (Su-U), the indivisible ki of the universe; Takami musubi no kami (A), the deity of yang ki expanding; and Kami musubi no kami (Wa), the deity of yin ki contracting. From within the kototama of Su, the life power draws in the breath of Yi, and water ki stands up vertically.

Expansion begins as Takami musubi no kami; the water ki of A rises up as the power of contrast (Ta). Ka gathers this ki together and turns it into power. Musubi is the blending together of fire (Ka) and water (Mi) ki.

The third deity, Kami musubi no kami, is created when the fire ki of Wa reaches out horizontally. The kototama of Ka connects these two energies, which then begin their function of cycling around each other to create a spiral form. Within this pattern, fire ki begins to sink down toward the center.

Passing diagonally through the center, the *katakana,* or letter, for the kototama of To is created. This entire process creates the *omote,* or basic form of Ikkyo, the first technique of Aikido. It is water ki rising and fire ki branching out to lead the form of the technique.

When this symbol is duplicated in all the eight directions, a flower of eight petals is created. It is an ancient symbol of Buddhism and Shinto, as well as Christianity. This symbol represents the way of governing without force, the principle of *suberu.* When the fire

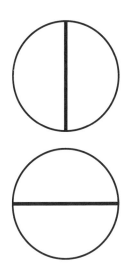

■ *Fig. 1.10. Symbols for Takami musubi and Kami musubi*

■ *Fig. 1.11. The sign of To*

■ Fig. 1.12. Flower of eight petals

and water ki of all seventeen deities have been combined in this way, the axis of time and space (I-Wi) is stabilized, and the creation of the manifest world can begin.

Building the levels of our consciousness is the same as building the levels of our life force field. It is much like the creation of a magnet. As fire and water ki, layer upon layer, wind around each other, they stabilize the center and the power of electromagnetic energy increases. This winding around the center is called *karami*, being the spiral (Ra) interchange of fire (Ka) and water (Mi) ki. It is also called the dance of the gods, or *kami*, yet this is a poetic expression of the Japanese race and does not indicate the existence of any actual deity.

Combining the vertical and horizontal ki of Takami musubi no kami and Kami musubi no kami, the first spiritual form is created. This is the cross, or ame no uki hashi, the floating bridge of heaven. *Ame*, once again, is the cycling of consciousness. *Uki* is the floating ki of the universe. Uki should be interpreted as *uku*, which is the vertical ki of water. *Hashi* is the horizontal ki of fire. Hashi also means the eight (*ha*) words (*shi*) that branch out as the power of recognition.

As fire and water continue to cycle around each other, the cross of ame no uki hashi is finally stabilized as I and Wi, the life will and power. From the intersection of these two, the eight directions of ki shoot forth in all directions and the manifest world comes forth in an instant.

In ancient Shinto, ame no uki hashi was understood as the intersection of Heaven's and Earth's ki, the cross of *tate* and *yoko*. Tate is vertical and yoko is horizontal. Yoko should be seen as the cross threads in weaving. In other words, it must always be subsidiary to tate. This is the essence of Aikido principle.

Tate and yoko comprise the invisible structure behind both mind and matter. It is the essence of Aikido principle, and therefore the foundation for the movement of our mind and our body. Unless this is seen clearly, the principle of Aikido and the way of manifesting it will be mistaken or missed altogether.

■ *Fig. 1.13. Ame no uki hashi and ame no hashi date*

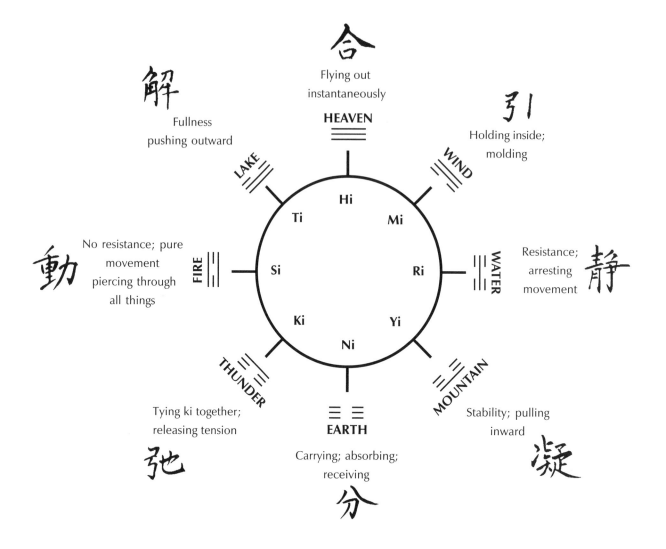

合
Flying out
instantaneously
HEAVEN

解
Fullness
pushing outward

引
Holding inside;
molding

LAKE

WIND

動
No resistance; pure
movement
piercing through
all things

FIRE

静
Resistance;
arresting
movement

WATER

Hi

Ti

Mi

Si

Ri

Ki

Yi

Ni

弛
Tying ki together;
releasing tension

THUNDER

MOUNTAIN

凝
Stability; pulling
inward

分
Carrying; absorbing;
receiving

EARTH

■ *Fig. 1.14. The eight powers*

As mentioned above, ame no hashi date, the standing bridge of Heaven, is the vertical ki created by our first in breath. This establishes the life will and power, I and Wi, as our center or one point. Breathing out from this place again, our ki is sent in the eight directions and polarity is established as the ki of yin and yang or fire and water. With each cycle of breath we continually create the eight powers.

WORD	DEITY	POWER
Ti	Uhijine	Pushing horizontally outward from the center
Yi	Suhijine	Pulling inward and reaching upward
Ki	Tsunugui	Releasing tension and tying ki together
Mi	Ikugui	Holding ki inside and molding it into form
Si	Ohotonoji	Pure, unrestricted movement; nonresistance
Ri	Ohotonobe	Resistance creating spiral form
Hi	Omotaru	Pure spirit; creative power flying out instantaneously
Ni	Kakashikone	Body; carrying, absorbing, receiving

All power is the result of the movement of universal spirit. Outside of this, there is no power. This movement is divided into eight aspects. The movement of universal spirit is *hikari,* invisible light wave vibration. "Everything that vibrates and radiates is called *hikari,* which means the 'running (*kari*)' of 'spirit (*hi*).' When the light of mind and the light of matter are synchronized, all phenomena appear. The eight father vibrations work as the basic elements of reality."[14]

■ *Fig. 1.15. Celtic cross*

Ti-Yi: The Power of Kokyu

Uhijine no kami and Suhijine no kami represent the kototama of Ti and Yi. *Uhiji* is written with the characters for universe-compare-earth, or the contrast between spirit and body. The U of Uhijine means "descending spiral." It is the root (Ne) of spirit (Ti) coming forth as instinct, or primitive mind.

The ki of Ta Ti Tsu Te To produces the fullness of each dimension. With our first in breath (Yi), the ki of Heaven and Earth are brought to our one point. With our exhalation (Ti) this ki is then pushed out horizontally. Fire ki pushing outward gives vitality to the blood in our hara and promotes wisdom in our spirit. In this way, the cross of tate and yoko is created.

Suhijine is Yi, the immovable root of wisdom rising up vertically like a mountain and rooting us in both Heaven and Earth. The kototama of Ya Yi Yu Ye Yo all have the quality of standing in the center as earth ki and unifying fire and water ki. The pure spirit of the universe is the creative breath of Hi. This kototama radiating outward to infinity is polarized into I and Wi, the life will and power. In order for creation to begin, however, these two must again be united. This unification is accomplished through the in breath of Yi.

When we draw breath inward (Yi), the original spark of life (Ti) is activated and begins to expand by pushing on its own center. This is the power of *kokyu* (breath), the fullness of wisdom pushing on itself and thereby creating Ta, the power of contrast. Similarly, the breath of Yi opens up as Ya, the beginning of self-consciousness. Together Ti and Yi become the first movement within the cross of tate and yoko.

Practice drawing your breath to your one point with the voice of Yi. Follow this by pushing on your own center to create the power of kokyu. The meeting point of Yi and Ti is the point of the greatest spiritual tension. In this way you should study drawing your partner's ki into your own center with a very slight in breath. Let your partner's power root you to the earth.

When you use the visualization power of your mind in this way, the power of unification grows together with faith in your own center, the kototama of I. Yi-Ti is the image of a man standing between and

■ *Fig. 1.16.* Kurai dachi:
*man standing in the
position between Heaven
and Earth (with sword)*

uniting Heaven and Earth. Pushing on others leads to defeat, yet pushing on yourself leads to wisdom.

Ti-Yi, the power of kokyu and stabilization, should first be practiced as *tai-atari,* or full body contact, a complete and direct meeting of mind and body. When the stability of Yi and the kokyu power of Ti are grasped as one unified function, your partner will be thrown backward the moment he makes contact with you.

The greater the power of your expanding ki, the more you will become rooted to your own center and to the earth. The more strongly your partner pushes on your body, the more you will be able to realize the source of your power as the earth itself. You should be able to move your partner's body as easily as if it were your own.

It is a characteristic of Eastern philosophy that the first and most basic teaching also contains the secret of mastery. With your very first breath, practice total unity through the power of kokyu. In the beginning this is very physical, yet it leads to ki development and the wisdom of Aikido.

**Aikitama: The Spirit of
Universal Harmony**

Ki-Mi: Connecting and Holding Inside— The Beginning of Form

Ki and Mi are represented by the deities of Tsunugui no kami and Ikugui no kami. *Tsunu* here relates to the word *tsunagu,* which means "to tie (the ki) together," thereby allowing it to continue (*tsutsuku*). *Gui* is the bringing together of two elements of spiritual ki. The deity for the kototama of Mi is Ikugui no kami. *Iku* is written with the ideogram for life. The hidden meaning, however, is <u>*iki wo kumu,*</u> "tying the breath of life (ki) together." This is the power of ki-musubi in Aikido.

When the great tension of universal ki is released in relative time and space, movement and form are created. This is the first turning of the cross as it becomes the wheel of materialization. It is shown in the ancient symbol called the *manji.* In the original Sanskrit, it was called a *sauvastica.* In the Japanese katakana syllabary, it is reduced to the letter for the kototama of Ka. It is the beginning of light in the world—the potential of materialization.

Ki is the medium through which we attach or focus our attention on any one thing. The kototama of Ka Ki Ku Ke Ko deals with tying ki together for the release of power as movement. O-sensei referred to these kototama as *sampeki,* the dragon that comes out of the East. Basically this is the beginning of dynamic interchange between yin and yang. It is like the release of an automobile clutch and the consequent engagement of the engine; there is a sudden burst of energy, power, and movement.

The ideograms for these two powers are pictures of a bowstring being pulled back and an arrow being released. As the kototama of Ki releases power, the rhythm of Mi maintains tension and holds ki inside. Understanding this feeling in your body, you are able to create ki-musubi, the tying of your ki together with that of your partner. This is fire and water ki, and its use determines the creation of form.

"Of all the forces that move things, none is swifter than thunder. Of all the forces that bend things, there is none more powerful than wind."[15] The kototama of Ki is the source of sensitivity, and when it is stimulated it releases power like thunder. The kototama of Mi is like the power of the wind. "The characteristic of this trigram is to make things flow into their forms, to make them conform to the shape prefigured by the seed."[16]

■ *Manji symbol and katakana symbol for Ka*

■ *Fig. 1.17. Releasing the tension of a partner's resistance*

The greatest tension of ki is at the center of our hara. This is mental awareness; to interpret it as physical tightness is a mistake. This holding ki inside is the voice of Mi. At the moment of contact with uke, ki is released, yet we should release only ten or fifteen percent. Holding the greater majority of our ki inside creates much more dynamic power. This is sometimes practiced with *ki-ai,* or shouting, yet it also should be studied in releasing power silently.

Aikitama: The Spirit of Universal Harmony

The nature of fire ki is adherence, catching onto things and tenaciously clinging to them. Alternating between the index finger (water) side of your hand and the little finger (fire) side, you should be able to move your partner either backward or forward and control his center.

Ki and Mi are manifest mainly through the movement of the hands and arms; as such, they are the main tools in the creation of form. This is *jutai,* the training of sensitivity and flexibility. The sensitivity of your touch causes a natural release of power and molds ki into form. Depending on the sensitivity of your touch, read your partner's intention at the moment of contact. Opening your hand brings his ki inside and releases your own ki outward.

In order to overcome physical strength with flexibility, it is necessary to distinguish between fire and water ki in movement. It is impossible to establish the correct flow of ki if your form is incorrect. If the orderly progression of fire ki leading water ki is neglected in your movement, the secrets of Aikido technique will not be revealed to you, regardless of how much you train.

Si-Ri: Piercing Through and Winding Around

The nature of Si and Ri is shown in the names of the representative deities, Ohotonoji no kami and Ohotonobe no kami. *Oho* means *dai,* or greatness. This is the power of movement from which all things are born. *Tono* is a term of the highest respect. It means "lord" or "ruler," the deity presiding over a shrine.

Si and Ri are the completion or final establishment of both form and feeling. As Ti-Yi is very much physical and Ki-Mi creates sensitive feeling, Si-Ri is the realm of consciousness, the final product of our spirit and soul. Si is *omou,* which has the dual meaning of "weight" and "thought."

The descending or concentration of our ki manifests consciousness as mana, thought, and inspiration. In Tibetan mysticism this is the root syllable Om or Aum. The final sound, *ji,* is written with the letter for earth. In other words, it is the foundation of all that is destined to become greatness.

Ohotonobe, the deity of Ri, is defined by the kototama of He or Be, which means "discernment," "reasonableness," or "balance." The kototama of To, in this case, means "to judge the value of things," or

■ *Fig. 1.18. Si-Ri in Katate tori shiho nage*

hakaru. The power of Ri is called *shizumeru,* meaning to "calm down," "to use the power of reason," or "to bring things under control."

Ri is also read *kotowari,* which literally means "the principle of the word" or "pure reason." Cutting to the chase, Si is our spiritual antennae, that which allows intuitive perception. Ri is the power of reason, that which makes that consciousness effective. Manifest as form, it is a spiral, the completed form of *ryutai* techniques.

Manifesting Aikido principle as suberu, or the spiral form of technique, is to bring forth the kototama of Si and Ri. Si, piercing through the center, and Ri, turning that ki into spiral form, are exemplified on the preceding page in the Shiho nage technique. These two energies working together turn the entire body into one effective spiral movement.

Aikido at the ryutai level is practical, economical, and graceful. Ryutai techniques manifest the precision judgment of E dimension's ki, balancing form and feeling spontaneously in the moment. If your judgment is sharp and accurate, your form will be expedient and your feeling will be completely alive, yet without physical tightness.

The kototama of Sa Si Su Se So are the ki of nonresistance, and therefore smooth, swift, and speedy movement. To manifest this feeling in your practice means to pass through your partner's resistance without meeting it at all. This is a high level of mastery. The kototama of Ra Ri Ru Re Ro are the power of receiving your partner's power and molding it into effective spiral form.

This is the meaning of *tai-sabaki,* or judgment in motion. This molding must always manifest the spiral principle of Aikido. If there is any manipulation, the kototama of Ri is lost. Ri is the fulcrum of creation. If our efforts lack principle, they will be ineffetive; there will be no joy or freedom in our lives.

To the degree that we manifest the ki of Si and Ri, our movement travels in larger and larger spirals, never losing control. Thus the movement of a master appears to be very direct yet never meets with a collision of force.

Si is like a master blade thrust through the wind. Ri is the subtle control of the blade, which comes from deep inside our center. It is the unfettered mind moving freely through delusion.

It is said that O-sensei used to whisper the sound of Su as he moved through his techniques. I often noticed Yamaguchi sensei, my own teacher, as he entered the mat. He seemed to breath outward slowly, barely audibly, with the sound of Su, bringing his mind and senses to a peaceful state before practice.

We should remember that the principle of movement is the principle of mind. Do not undervalue the power of mind. It is our ability to create an image of beauty and effectiveness that makes such a manifestation possible. The word for creation is *souzou*. It also means "the power of thought," yet this thought must be based on reality, rather than mere imagination, if it is to be effective.

Hi-Ni: Creative Power—Receiving Power

In Shinto the kototama of Hi is called Omotaru no kami, and that of Ni is Ayakashikone no kami. Omotaru is the deity who continually gives out everything yet remains perfect and complete. *Omo* is *omote,* which means "all things revealed" or "nothing hidden." *Taru* is "to be sufficient." It is to be perfect and complete as you are, with nothing lacking. Ayakashikone's name means "the root" (*ne*) of "wisdom, reverence, and grace" (*kashiko*) manifest into "form" (*aya*).

There can be no arrogance or haughtiness here, no idea of knowing. The spirit of Hi-Ni is acting in accordance with the dictates of the moment, not a self-appointed mission. True wisdom is in selfless action, not in great words or teachings. The words of Lao Tsu should be remembered: "The leader with absolute virtue works subtly. He helps all people, yet the people are barely aware of his existence."[17]

The rhythms of Hi and Ni are also called the powers of unification (*goryoku*) and separation (*bunryoku*). Goryoku is the combination of all forces; bunryoku, which in Japanese is defined as "a component of a force," is a part that contains the essence of the whole. Unification here refers to the state of inexhaustible spiritual ki—the function of Ha Hi Hu He Ho. This ki, reaching out to the extremities of the universe in a moment, becomes the power of recognition, distinguishing subject and object, and manifesting the world. As we saw above, the life will and power (I-Wi) appear as the subjective and objective sides of the rhythm of Hi, or pure spirit.

The kototama of Hi is the pure spirit of fire encircling the heavens and manifesting as the circle of the sun. In contrast, the spirit of water (Mi) is associated with the moon and becomes the ki through which the life power (Wi) controls the tides of the earth.

Hi is spirit, or ki, as the true body. It is to move your entire being as spirit and ki. This must be understood before small movement can be effective. For the master, this whole body movement can be expressed

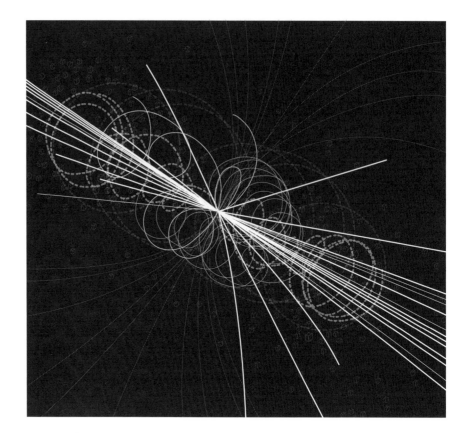

■ *Fig. 1.19. The first particle of life*

merely by moving the little finger. "Every part equals the whole." This is Ni, or *bunryoku*, the power of the parts. It is for this reason that the master seems to move very little yet can never be restrained.

In the world of pure spirit (Hi), creation begins with the birth of subject and object. The breath of Heaven (Ha) reaches out to the infinite universe, giving birth to A and Wa. It reaches out to the extremities of the universe in a moment, and there it radiates as the light of ki. "And God separated the light from the darkness."[18]

This is the light of consciousness. It is not the light we see, but the light by which we see. The first particle of light and mind should not be understood as something outside of ourselves. As it happens in Heaven and on Earth, so, too, it happens within every aspect of our being.

When the creation is completed, mankind, giving birth to wisdom, stands at the center and unifies all seeming dichotomies. This is the kototama of Ya Yi Yu Ye Yo. In this way the beginning and the end are once again united. The creative power of Ha Hi Hu He Ho leads back, once again, to Yi-Ti, the stabilization of ki in the form of the cross. When the creative power of Hi becomes rooted in Ni, the absorbing power of the earth, it is the complete intimacy of body and spirit.

This is the manifestation of divine light in the human form, the ultimate meaning of Logos. Ni may also be interpreted as *ninau,* or carrying. The reverent humility and grace of Ni shine forth in the figure of Kannon sama, the goddess of mercy who hears the cries of the world and responds immediately.

The row of Na Ni Nu Ne No is the essence of body and the earth. It is the meeting point of breathing in and out. Breathing in with the kototama of Yi, we bring ki to our center. Carrying that ki with the kototama of Ni, the technique unfolds. Finally, breathing out, we release all tension and follow our partner's descent. This is the basis of Aikido kokyu training.

The rhythms of Hi and Ni relate to *kitai* practice. In the *kotai* training of Ti-Yi, we emphasize the whole body contact of attacks like *ryote tori.* In the *jutai* training of Ki-Mi, our contact rotates between our handblade and the index-finger side of our hand, never placing full contact against our palm, which is earth ki.

In the *ryutai* training of Si-Ri, we practice suberu, sliding through, almost not touching, and merging with our partner's movement. This is also whole body connection, yet it is very different from the *tai-atari* of kotai training. Arriving at the mastery level of Hi-Ni, our contact is that of mind alone.

The contact of Hi-Ni should be immediate and nonphysical. Receive and influence your partner's ki with your own mind and ki even before contact is made. To manifest Hi and Ni is to be the most sensitive receiver of uke's energy.

In order for kitai training to be successful, we must understand unity from the beginning. We move freely and harmoniously, manifesting the spiral form of *irimi-tenkan.* This ability must be well grounded in kotai, jutai, and ryutai training if it is to have any practical reality.

■ *Fig. 1.20. Kannon of light (painting by Daniel doAmaral)*

■ *Fig. 1.21. Four examples of kitai waza—leading uke's mind with hara alone*

2 ■ SANGEN

The Unique Principle of Dynamic Monism

■ *Sangen*　三元

DYNAMIC MONISM

The word *principle* has been used to denote rules, theories, and sometimes even an attitude or opinion, yet there is only one principle that governs all things. It is called "the unique principle." It is the principle by which all things in the natural world function. In Japanese Shinto it is called *sangen,* the three origins represented by the symbols of the triangle, the circle, and the square.

The triangle represents forward movement beginning from a single point and reaching outward. The circle is created by the continuation of that movement and therefore is actually all manifest movement and the form that it creates. The square represents the stability of one point reaching outward in the eight directions. The combination of these three aspects creates suberu, the spiral principle of Aikido.

The word *suberu* has the dual meaning of "to slide" and "to govern" or "to control." Su is the ki of nonresistance, and Ru is the resistance that molds that ki into vibration and spiral form. The kototama of Be is created from He, which indicates a perfect balance between tate and yoko, the eight powers. It is this balance that allows you to slide through the movement without meeting your partner's resistance.

In a word, the unique principle is the threefold function of dynamic monism.* Its visible appearance is the working of yin and yang, or fire and water ki, yet its essence transcends both relative and absolute. In Buddhism and in Aikido, the principle governing this threefold reality is represented specifically by the symbol of the triangle. O-sensei described it as follows: *The polarization of U is the beginning of dharma, or universal law. This is the divine mystery (*himitsu*) of universal function.*

Sangen, or the three origins, is always in a state of becoming. When the infinite expansion of A dimension is born from Mu-Su-U, there is nothing but expansion. This is absolute. Due to this expansion meeting itself, there is also expansion and contraction, or relativity, within the absolute. It can therefore be called neither relative nor absolute.

One of the basic precepts of Buddhism is "practice good, do not create evil." In other words, there is no such thing as inherent evil. In essence the universe and nature are 100 percent positive, and it is only due to our relative perspective that negativity is perceived. On the other hand, there is no possibility of an absolute or perfect existence outside of its relative manifestation.

Without the tools of polarity, even the absolute could not create anything. In this way we should understand fire and water ki to be the right and left hands of God. They are called *himitsu,* or the secret of the universe. This secret is the principle of fire (Hi) and water ki (*mitsu* or *mizu*).

In order for fire and water ki, the active ingredients of movement, to perform their function, they must be continually born from earth ki, the infinite source. This continual birth of life is principle; it is the great secret of life because its function cannot be grasped through the intellect. In the words of Zen Master Dogen, "Practice is enlightenment." There is no true knowing outside of immediate experience or practice.

The basis of reality is the third dimension. It is within the third dimension that all other dimensions exist. Within this continual and dynamic movement, the perfect balance of opposites can never occur;

---

*The principle of dynamic monism indicates that there is no such thing as a separate entity in nature or the universe and that all things are interdependent and in constant motion.

therefore the cross of tate and yoko, or fire and water ki, is always in motion. Reality is never complete. It is always in a state of becoming. It is always two plus something, yet never three.

The three points of the triangle are traditionally represented by the elements of fire, water, and earth. Represented by the cross these are tate, yoko, and center. In Aikido we understand earth as the unified source, and fire and water as the polarization, or yin and yang, of that all-encompassing origin. Fire ki draws inward and leads the movement. Water ki pushes outward, following and supporting that lead.

Earth ki is the ki of hara, the origin of movement. In movement, however, it is already divided into fire and water ki. Although fire ki draws inward, its appearance is active and centrifugal. Although water ki pushes ki outward, its appearance is passive and centripetal. Earth ki is the source, yet it is also the final product, the body itself. The Shinto teaching is *reishu, shinju, taizoku,* or spirit leading, mind following, and body attached. Nevertheless, spirit and body are interdependent and mutually arising. If we consider them as one, they are already two. If we see them as two, they are already the threefold function of oneness. The reality of essence cannot be grasped by the conceptual mind.

In Japan, the famous and beautiful Mount Fuji is a symbol of this principle; its cone shape clearly shows how the triangle form is seen as the two sides of one indivisible reality. The name Fuji may be interpreted to mean "no two." We see two sides, yet we cannot see the threefold reality from any one perspective.

Two is a wheel without an axle; it can go nowhere. It is a philosophical explanation of an ungraspable reality. The third factor is the eternally unborn. It is the ultimate reality of the manifest, from which perception occurs. It can be realized only when the self is forgotten. At that time it is heard in the sound of the river flowing, a bird crying out, or a distant road being traveled.

Without this source, the principle of fire and water, yin and yang, or tate and yoko becomes dualistic and void of spiritual content or practical value. Conceptual explanations can never grasp it. Principle must be grasped within practice as dynamic unity. We should be very clear about the essential unity of all things.

The Tao Te Ching states, "The way begets one; one begets two;

■ *Fig. 2.1. Mount Fuji (painting by Katsumi Sugita)*

two begets three; three begets the myriad creatures."[1] This is easily misinterpreted to mean that the manifest is born from a preexisting essence, yet that essence is no different from that which it produces. Life continually creates polarity within the great universal void and then unifies it by standing between the two sides. It is a beginning that is without beginning, and therefore also without an end.

Even if it were possible to have an ocean without waves, it is impossible to have waves without the ocean. Even if it were possible to have plains without mountains and valleys, it is not possible to have mountains and valleys without the earth. Our very existence here and now, as nature questioning itself, stands as proof of the ultimate unity of an origin continually giving birth to itself in ever more evolved form.

In order to grasp a reality that is always in motion we must see both sides of any equation. Those who hold rigidly to one side or another cannot find the center upon which realization depends. The separation of relative and absolute is created by the limitations, or boundaries, of our own imperfect perception.

Even Jesus Christ, the great sage of Christianity, refused to speculate on the origin: "If the flesh has come into being because of the

■ *Kannagara no michi*

■ *Miki*

spirit, it is a marvel. But if the spirit has come into being because of the body, it is a marvel of marvels. But I marvel at how this great wealth has made its home in this poverty."[2]

Sangen, the unique principle, is the foundation of all of our major religious traditions. This teaching is ancient, dating back to Kannagara no michi, the original Shinto. It was passed down as the cosmology of the ancient sun-worshipping race and reached India around 400 BCE. In Hinduism it was expressed as the trinity of Shiva, Brahma, and Vishnu. These, in turn, symbolize the kototama of U, A, and Wa.

This is perhaps the earliest record of what was to become the Christian trinity. Christianity calls it the Father, the Son, and the Holy Ghost. The Father is the creative force of Heaven, the Son is mankind, and the Holy Ghost is what Buddhists call *dharma,* the laws of universal movement. In other words the Holy Ghost is the entire manifest world and also the laws governing its movement.

The Taoist expression of sangen is *ten, jin,* and *chi,* or Heaven, man, and Earth. This also may be expressed as spirit, mind, and body. Considered separately, each of these is absolute in and of itself. For this reason, they are represented by the simplest form that can be drawn with straight, or absolute, lines.

THE FUNCTION OF KI

Earth ki, or *tsuchi no ki,* is the ki of the center. In our body it is the hara, the source of both our ki and our blood. This is the point from which life and movement begins. Water ki, or *mizu no ki,* is feminine and relates to the earth. This is the ki of materialization. Mizu no ki abbreviated to *miki* means the right, or more physical, side of the body. This ki is predominant in woman, who draws it upward from the earth to create her yang essence. Moving to the right this ki becomes a clockwise spiral of materialization. This is the water ki of the moon rising in the east.

Hi no ki, or fire ki, is masculine and relates to Heaven. Hi no ki relates to the left side of the body and is called *hitari.* Fire ki is strongest in man, who draws it downward from Heaven to create his yin essence. Moving to the left it becomes the counterclockwise spiral of spiritualization. This is the fire ki of the sun sinking in the west.

Although the right side of the body is originally water ki, it becomes fire ki when movement is initiated from the right side. Sitting before the Aikido shrine we place our hands together. Dropping the right hand down until our fingers rest on our palm, we place the left hand, the spiritual side, in the dominant position.

Next we take our right hand and strike our left. The right hand in stillness is water ki, yet here it initiates movement and therefore takes the role of fire ki. Our left, which is normally fire ki, receives the strike and produces the sound of clapping. Therefore, in this case, it becomes water ki.

When fire and water are seen as the five elements, the result is the same. From the teachings of Yamaguchi Shido: *In other words, wood is water ki and metal is the ki of fire. Striking metal with wood, metal becomes water and creates sound. Striking wood with metal, wood returns to its original nature and produces sound.* Principle should be researched in this way for Aikido training.

Principle is the threefold function of universal spirit, the kototama of Su. Fire and water ki are active and apparent. Earth ki is the manifest world, yet its essence always remains hidden. It is like history; it has no existence except as it manifests through particular laws, events, and examples. Earth ki, nevertheless, unifies all laws and events, including the seeming dichotomy of relativity and absolute itself.

■ *Hitari*

THE SPIRIT AND FORM OF PRINCIPLE

The pure ki of fire is without form; this is the body of fire. The pure ki of water is without form; this is the body of water. The universal body is without boundaries. Fire and water ki, each in and of itself, fill the entire universe without interrupting each other. This is the subjective reality of pure spirit. It is undivided ki without the slightest gap.

It is from this polarity that the movement of the body begins. *Fire ki moves and water ki is moved.* Drawing inward and creating a center, movement begins with the breath of fire ki. When there is movement there is ki, mind, and form. Without movement, even rocks and mountains would disappear from the face of the earth.

In the words of Zen master Dogen, "If you doubt the walking of

Sangen: The Unique Principle
of Dynamic Monism

mountains, it is because you do not know your own walking. If you want to understand your own walking, you must also understand the walking of these green mountains. If this walking had ever stopped, the Buddhas and ancestors could not appear."[3]

Movement begins with intention, and that is created by our will. With our first in breath, the kototama of Yi, the ki of Heaven and Earth are drawn into our one point and unified. "The power should be evenly distributed into the hips and the hara. . . . By unifying both into one, the correct center of power is generated. It passes through the spinal nerves from the sacral nerve plexus, and stops the working of the ideation center of the cerebrum."[4]

When our mind is securely focused in our one point, there is only intuitive perception and we receive our partner's force in one point. This makes unity possible. If our mind goes to the place where our partner attacks, the flow of ki and breath stops and physical tension is created. This makes unification impossible.

When the form of fire is revealed, this is water within fire and its function of burning begins. When the form of water is revealed, this is fire within water and its function of flowing begins. The function of burning here means the movement of ki and mind. The function of flowing refers to physical movement. It is our ki that moves and our body that is subsequently moved. Movement of either body or mind is always a blend of fire and water ki.

Movement begins from our hara, and especially our one point, yet this should be the the movement of mind and breath. When we truly are centered in one point, our mind does not wander and our faith is firm. In this case the movement of our mind alone may be sufficient to control a situation even before it begins. With one point remaining the center of tate and yoko, we are automatically led to discover correct form.

Standing between and receiving the ki of Heaven and Earth, the form of tate and yoko reaches out from our one point. Standing in the center and balancing all opposites is the practice of standing on ame no uki hashi, the floating bridge of Heaven. This is the proper way of working with the eight powers. When the principle of tate and yoko is maintained, spiral form, the kototama of Ru, or Ryu, comes forth in our movement and technique.

■ *Fig. 2.2. The balance of the opposing spirals, the kototama of Ru (Ryu) (from Matsuzo Hamamoto, Bansei Ikkei no Genri to Hanya Shingyo no Nazo)*

Sangen: The Unique Principle of Dynamic Monism

■ *Tate*

■ *Yoko*

■ *Fig. 2.3. Cross of tate and yoko over the human body*

TATE AND YOKO IN MOTION AND FORM

Attempting to create the form of technique directly, you will inevitably fall into the mistake of manipulation. The correct form of Aikido should be born through the maintenance of tate and yoko in motion. The Aikido of a master takes place inside the body and is accomplished by one movement of mind alone. It cannot be seen by the uninitiated. "I believe that it cannot be said that one's Aikido is genuine unless one's technique looks false to the eyes of the observer."[5]

TATE	YOKO
Main	Secondary
Mental connection	Physical connection
Spirit (unification)	Body (separation)
Straight lines	Curved lines
Fire ki in stillness	Water ki in stillness
Water ki in motion	Fire ki in motion
Vertical (rising and sinking)	Horizontal (turning)
Linear (*irimi*)	Circular (*tenkan*)
Extension	Turning
Direct (*yang-omote*)	Indirect (*yin-ura*)

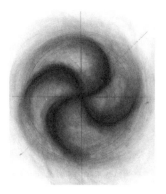

■ *Fig. 2.4. Cursive cross over vertical, horizontal, and diagonal lines*

With the in breath and the out breath, the cross of tate and yoko begins to turn and the motivating power of movement is born. Tate and yoko begin to cycle and change position and the cursive cross of fire and water ki is born. *The ki of fire is originally in the heavenly realm, yet branching outward it sinks down to the earth. The ki of water is originally of the earth, yet rising upward it cycles in the heavens.*

With each in breath the life will draws the straight lines of I dimension's ki into your center. With each out breath the cursive form of both mind and matter is expressed. In your movement the straight lines of I dimension's ki should run through and support the curved lines of visible form, the realm of E dimension. To the degree that you manifest the straight lines of I dimension's ki in your feeling, your form comes forth in ever larger spirals of increasing beauty and effectiveness (see fig. 3.26 on page 104).

Centering your mind in your one point, and reaching upward with the crown of your head, your body should be free of tension, yet your ki should be tight (at tension), connecting to your partner without any gap whatsoever. The mental tension of your focus should sink deep into your center and also extend to your fingertips, the periphery of your body. In this way your physical body is relaxed and supported by your kokyu, and your partner is unable to enter into your space.

■ *Fig. 2.5. Fire branches down to Earth, water rises up to Heaven.*

One point, or tanden no ichi, is not a physical organ; it has no physical counterpart. It is the center of ki in the body, and its effectiveness depends on your awareness and the degree of faith that you have in it. Keeping your focus in your one point regardless of outside opposition is extremely difficult, yet this is one of the most important parts of Aikido training. This is the meaning of real faith. The more deeply you are rooted in one point, the more the power of I dimension increases.

In the process of gradually developing this faith, it is necessary to continually study the balance between tate and yoko, between fire and water ki. When this dynamic balance becomes naturally correct in the moment, the obstruction to receiving in one point is removed and you receive continual feedback from your partner's attack. Depending on this feedback, the wisdom of I dimension becomes more deeply rooted in your center. Regardless of the degree of your partner's power, keep your mind in your one point, extend ki to your fingertips, and do not allow tension in your arms.

Controlling the subtle balance between vertical and horizontal motion depends on being centered in one point. You must unify with your partner's power before you can give it a new direction. A perfect response can arise only as the result of being a perfect receiver. To the degree that you develop sensitive receptivity you will be able to spontaneously create a new direction toward freedom of movement.

The most basic rule of tate and yoko is that tate must always take priority over yoko. Tate is ame no hashi date, the unified spiritual ki of Heaven and Earth. Yoko distributes that ki as physical power. The source of Aikido power, therefore, is always on the vertical plane, yet the distribution of that power comes from the horizontal turning of the upper body. This must be subtle or the vertical source of this power will be destroyed.

Understanding this relationship, it should be clear that *above* always controls *below*. The relationship between above and below is a vertical one, yet control is exercised through horizontal movement. A leaf falling from a tree, for example, moves to the left and the right as it descends. In this same way, you will easily control your partner's body by moving it horizontally from above.

Body language does not lie. Your body movement and the way that you solve physical problems clearly reveal your perception of reality. If this were not the case, it would not be possible to affect deep spiritual change through the practice of Aikido. "Truth does not exist apart from form. Truth in form is reality."[6]

In the Aikido of a master, the rising and sinking of the body is virtually invisible; it has been internalized and is accomplished through mind alone. For the beginner or even intermediate student, however, this should be emphasized in all techniques until the vertical source of your kokyu power is clearly understood.

In Aikido the arms should not be allowed to exert physical effort in any direction whatsoever, yet your one point should work in all directions. Using your arms to lift or suppress your partner's body to the right, left, or in any direction whatsoever destroys the possibility of unification. The first spiral of Aikido is rising upward.

In stillness, such as in meditation or before movement, the vertical plane (tate) is active as fire ki. In motion it becomes water ki, the passive receiver. In this case your forward movement (tate) becomes fire ki, and the turning of the body (yoko) becomes water ki.

Basically, one person has just as much ki as another, yet the power

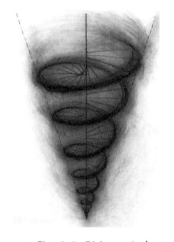

■ *Fig. 2.6. Rising spiral*

■ *Fig. 2.7. Rising spiral of Katate tori irimi kokyu nage*

■ *Fig. 2.8. Entering with Katate tori irimi*

of your concentration increases its effectiveness. It is how you hold your ki and direct it that matters. Inhaling slightly with the voice of Wi, sink your body (tate) and draw uke's ki into your center. At the moment of unification, send your ki into the common space between you. The slight turning of your waist turns uke's body away from you and sends his ki upward in an ascending spiral.

Simply rising, sinking, and turning the body is the first example of tate and yoko movement. If you master this way of moving and feeling, you will be able to cause uke's ki to rise upward regardless of what kind of contact you have with him. Rising upward, his balance becomes weak, and the natural weight of your body will be sufficient to bring uke down. If vertical ki is not predominant over the turning of your body, you will lose your connection with uke and your technique will inevitably fail.

The second tate-yoko relationship is that of forward motion and turning, or *irimi-tenkan*. In this case fire ki becomes the spirit of irimi entering directly into your partner's attack, and the turning of your waist releases power as water ki. Irimi is the basic spirit of Aikido.

Sangen: The Unique Principle of Dynamic Monism

■ *Fig. 2.9. Morote irimi nage: leading uke by your grasped hand*

Tenkan should be understood as the continuation of irimi, rather than as a movement unto itself.

In order to be effective there must always be yang within yin and yin within yang. Irimi is not successful without a certain degree of tenkan, and vice versa. The hand that leads the movement is fire ki and draws ki inward. The hand of water is a stronger physical connection and sends ki outward. Your two hands as a unit, however, should lead the ki out of uke's body. The focus of your hara balances this by continually sending ki directly into uke's hara as you pass through the movement.

In the *morote tori* technique, for example, your partner grasps your one arm with both of his. If you push into his power with your arm, you will lose. Rather you should use the fire mudra to lead his ki out of his body while receiving his ki in your own. In this way you can use uke's power to raise your own arm.

The third important example of tate and yoko is the movement of the arms. Balancing the yin and yang of the hands requires, once again, that tate remain dominant over yoko. The natural movement of the arms includes only extension, retraction (tate), and turning (yoko). If the balance of fire and water ki in your arms is correct, your partner will fall freely, as if in a vacuum.

The hand of fire (*hi no te*) and the hand of water (*mizu no te*) alternate as the dominant factors in the technique, yet fire always leads the movement. The hand of fire is active and controls uke's mind by seeking his center, or vulnerable point, where *atemi* can be applied. This is a physically fragile connection and therefore cannot be used successfully for power. In your feeling, however, this is the most substantial and important connection.

The hand of water is a physical connection and therefore should not be used for power. It should be seen as insubstantial. It exists only as a bridge or passive conductor, riding on the periphery of the movement. This bridge makes it possible to establish a hara-to-hara connection with uke. In summary, neither arm should be used for power.

Hara is earth ki, the source of fire and water ki, yet even this power, once again, should amount to only a few ounces of physical pressure on uke's body. After all, our one point has no power of its own. It relies completely on the power that is received from uke and then gives it a new direction. It is therefore said in the Chinese classics that three ounces of pressure should be able to move one thousand pounds. To the degree that the fire and water ki of the five dimensions and eight powers is properly balanced, there will be no need for unreasonable force.

Being able to move your partner's body with a minimum of pressure depends on being able to move his mind. If, for example, your physical contact occurs at your own and your partner's wrists, you should try to move his hara directly without interrupting the point of physical contact whatsoever. Uke will be unable to discover or defend against the source of your power. This kind of indirect pressure shows the triangle principle clearly.

There should be no attempt to control uke's body. Rather, control the space around his body. If you control the space around uke's body, he will be forced to move in order to avoid being vulnerable to a strike to his face or body.

One again, if tenkan, or turning, becomes divorced from tai-atari, the whole body contact created by forward inertia will be lost. It is the whole body connection of tai-atari that makes it possible for your arms to move freely. Unless you maintain direct hara-to-hara contact, your arms will receive uke's power and be unable to create the proper form of the technique.

This is the threefold working of fire, water, and earth, the principle of Aikido. As one function they are called simply *hara*. Thus the samurai maxim, "Do it with hara," has no hidden meaning; it means exactly what it says.

TATE-YOKO OF HACHIRIKI

When the eight powers are seen as eight directions, they are tate, yoko, and *naname,* or the diagonals. This is up-down, left-right, and the diagonals on both sides of the center. When we add inside and outside, we arrive at ten directions that must be simultaneously balanced in correct Aikido movement.

Rising and sinking on a vertical plane (tate) shows the kototama of Hi and Ni. This is controlled by the legs. Turning the body (yoko) is controlled by the waist. When these occur simultaneously the result is naname, the diagonal or spiral form of Aikido technique.

Done properly, the turning of the waist allows us to avoid direct conflict, and also to distribute the power of natural weight and concentration that we receive on the vertical plane. Moving forward with irimi-tenkan manifests the kototama of Si and Ri. Ti and Yi relate to the balance between inside and outside, the power of kokyu. Ki and Mi deal mainly with form and the maintenance of ki-musubi with your partner.

Maintaining the dynamic balance of the eight powers is essential in all Aikido techniques and movement. At the moment of direct whole body contact with your partner, the hands and hips will move in opposite directions. This should occur on both the vertical and the horizontal plane.

Sinking down and receiving should be on the vertical plane with

■ *Fig. 2.10. Drawing a sword shows the separation of hands and hips.*

your hips aligned to those of your partner. This is the omote position from which Aikido techniques begin. Rising up to meet your partner's power, hands and hips separate, moving in opposite directions. When you have gone beyond the difficulty your hips, once again, align with those of uke. In this way there is no collision of force, even at the moment of strongest contact.

If this momentary separation is visible, it is excessive. It should appear that the hips do not move at all. Done correctly, your hips will face into those of your partner from the beginning of the technique to the end of the movement.

O-sensei explained this balance in the simplest of terms: *Two plus eight equals ten. Four plus six equals ten. Five plus five equals ten.* Throughout this process, fire and water ki create the active interchange of the form, while earth ki functions as the stabilizing center. The function of *sangen hachi riki* is the working of fire and water ki unified by the ki of earth.

Studying principle as tate and yoko, we see the origin of form. In essence, Aikido can be divided into form and feeling. Feeling is the realm of ki, and therefore kokyu. Although the word *kokyu* is used constantly in Aikido, too often it is left vague, or not really practiced with a clear grasp of all its implications. The truth of the matter is that kokyu is the secret (*himitsu*) of Aikido. As with all spiritual disciplines, kokyu is at the root of the training. In Aikido it is kokyu that creates not only power and timing, but also the ability of unification, the trademark of Aikido.

The Breath of Life

▪ *Iki*

THE BREATH OF HEAVEN, EARTH, AND MAN

There is something that runs through all things, unifying them and giving them life. It is called *iki,* or the breath of life. The kototama of I is water ki and the kototama of Ki is fire ki. The substance of iki is kokyu, the pulse of the universe. All things that live do so by breath. The sun, the earth, and all things on the earth live, first of all, by breath. This is the starting point of our life, and of our endeavor to grasp its meaning.

The ki of the universe gives birth to us through breath and sustains its own creation through breath. Becoming consciously aware of breath, ki, and mind as our true body, the illusion of separation disappears and it becomes possible to manifest power far beyond that of physical muscle. If you realize this basic truth, you will be able to relax your body completely and still produce immovable power.

The infinitely expanding ki of the universe is polarized into the breath of Heaven and the breath of Earth. Once again from the *Kototama Hissho* of Yamaguchi Shido: *The cycling of the sun, moon, and stars is the breath of Heaven. The rising and falling of the tides is the breath of Earth. When the breath of Heaven and the breath of Earth are combined, all things are born. When the breath of human beings is unified, the ability of thought is born.*

Becoming aware of the trinity of breath, ki, and mind as your true body, the illusion of separation disappears. It should be understood that the breath of Heaven and Earth and the breath of human beings are the same. If you wish to grasp the principle of Heaven and Earth in its widest perspective, it is as close to you as your own breath.

The kokyu of Heaven and Earth and the kokyu of humans are basically the same. *As a universal function it is called* kami, *the ki of fire and water. In human beings it functions as* tamashihi, *our soul and spirit. The heart of a human being is no different from the soul of Heaven and Earth. Tama is spirit, Shi is water ki, and Hi is fire ki.* Breathing in, we feel the breath as coolness. This is water ki (I) rising due to the virtue of fire (Yi). *Fire burns by virtue of water; water flows by virtue of fire.*

Life begins with the silent inhalation. When a child is born, it is the in breath that expands the lungs in preparation for the first declaration of life as *gnnyaa*—the first cry. Breathing inward, we unify with our environment. Breathing out again, thought, language, and movement are born. In order to maintain the ki that has been taken in, the exhalation should be long and slow.

Fire ki moves, yet it has no voice. Water ki is moved, yet it gives voice to nature. When ocean waves draw back there is little sound, yet when they push forward, sound and great power come forth. The great trees in the forest voice their eerie creaking sound as they breathe out and release moisture. In both cases, this is the power of spirit, ki, or word.

Breathing inward, the breath silently follows the ki of fire. Releasing that breath, the ki of water manifests the power of physical movement and the creation of form. This is the first law of nature's creative process. Becoming conscious of the breath, you begin the path toward self-realization. Through breath, human will merges with that of the universe. The paradise was never lost, yet it is remembered for the first time.

Taking your first breath as a human being, you complete 2.8 billion years of evolution and step onto this earth as an amphibian in human form. When you complete your first set of teeth, you have reached the first level of a human being. Physical verticality takes several years to accomplish, yet the fulfillment of our spiritual potential requires a lifetime.

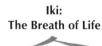

THREE STAGES OF KOKYU

The meaning of kokyu is not limited to physical breath; it also should be understood as the expansion and contraction of our ki, the pulse of life. Usually breathing is an automatic process, just like the beating of the heart, yet human beings have the ability to use kokyu to strengthen and direct the life force through concentration of mind.

Most simply, kokyu may be used to calm the five senses and deepen our perception. This is merging with the kototama of Su. This is a beginning point for progress in Aikido, and for spiritual growth in general. When this feeling becomes a part of our everyday sensory experience, it is the foundation of spiritual awakening.

As you become aware of the breath and its importance, you will go beyond the endless repetition of physical movements and gain true understanding. It is said in the Chinese classics that the mind leads the breath and the breath leads the ki. Practicing in this way, eventually you can learn to direct your ki by intention alone.

As we draw breath into one point and again release it, the circulation of our ki and the nourishment of our blood are replenished continually. Consciously drawing our mind to one point, we are led toward the discovery of wisdom. Kokyu is the way of unifying body and mind and merging with your partner. Quite frankly, it may be said that kokyu is the greater part of Aikido. It is the source of both power (*kokyu ryoku*) and timing. Timing in Aikido is not a matter of great speed, but rather the ability of ki-musubi, or tying your breath and ki together with that of your partner.

Kokyu is the first function of principle. It is the threefold process of receiving, carrying, and releasing ki. Breath and ki, like physical food, must be taken in and digested before being released. The intermediate stage of "carrying" the ki is essential to the ability of ki-musubi, or unity in motion.

Receiving begins even before contact. This should be the time of your greatest physical extension. As you make physical contact, draw your partner's ki to your center with your breath, as your arms contract. When your ki reaches your center, the stage of carrying begins and your arms extend from one point again.

■ *Fig. 3.1. Ryote kokyu nage: receiving, carrying, and releasing*

As your arms extend, your hips should move back and create space between you and your partner (1). In this way, the point of contact with your partner remains the same (2, 3). Releasing, the final stage, is simply letting go as you pass through the center of the movement (4). The carrying stage of kokyu, therefore, is essentially almost the totality of the movement.

This carrying of ki expresses the earth ki of Na Ni Ne No Nu, which stands at the center between the inhalation and the exhalation. The in breath is the fire ki of unification, and releasing the breath is water ki.

In Aikido you should learn to receive with the breath first, before the movement of the technique begins. The ability to not react immediately is very important. Your body may be in motion as you receive, yet there is a moment of almost stopping in order to let uke's power sink deeply into your hara. This should be done with the voice of Wi or Sui, drawing uke's ki inside like a vacuum. The sound of Wi is like a bottomless well, the source of life power.

The breath should be coordinated with the movement of the body. The breath moves slowly and rapidly, rising and sinking, yet never stopping altogether. Reaching out with your arms, breathe in and receive uke's ki. Carrying that ki and letting it sink deeply into your hara, move through the technique. Finally, when all difficulty has been removed, breathe outward and follow his descent to the mat.

As you learn to take in ki with your mind alone, the ingestion of ki can be continued throughout the technique. In other words, the "carrying" stage is lengthened. This allows the entire movement to be completed by ki-musubi alone. This is important in building the power of ki for both martial and spiritual progress.

In Aikido the out breath should be released slowly. Even in the case of a shout, or ki-ai, only a little air should be released. If the ki is exhausted, it will be difficult to adapt to the next movement. If you depend on physical strength to accomplish the technique, your kokyu will either stop or become chaotic, making readiness and meaningful response impossible.

In most martial arts, emphasis is placed on the out breath in order to create an explosion of sudden power. At the end of the out breath, however, it is impossible to react to a sudden attack. In sword training it is taught that you should attack when your partner finishes his out breath. This is at the end of the movement, before he can take an in breath to begin a new movement.

Contrary to the teaching of most martial arts, Aikido stresses the importance of the in breath for the purpose of unification. Unless that breath is taken into the hara, however, it may cause the ki to rise up the front of your body and thereby weaken your stability. Breathing into the hara allows you to accomplish whole body and mind unification with your partner. When this is done, his body will move as if it were your own.

The idea of trying to move another person's body is based on a dualistic, and therefore mistaken, perspective. It is an impossible task. Rather, create a direction toward freedom with your fingertips and move your hara freely. If your physical form conforms to your kokyu and intention, you will be able to move without hindrance.

KOKYU AS POWER AND TIMING

Seeing principle as an abstract idea is of little value. Understanding it as kokyu, however, you begin for the first time to grasp the reality of spirit and body as one. Drawing ki from the earth below and the heavens above, it arrives at the center of your hara. This completes the trinity of Heaven, man, and Earth.

When you unify these three factors, you will receive your partner's force in the earth and thereby borrow its power and stability. You will become immovable even while completely relaxed. Opening your hands, take in Heaven's ki and give it new direction. Power comes from the earth, the kototama of Umn (which equals Aum or Om). Direction (E) comes from the expansion of Heaven's ki (A).

As you use your breath to lead your ki through your limbs and to your hara, your legs will remain light and agile even while being rooted to the earth. The movement of the arms follows the breath. At the end of your physical extension, the breath has already began to pull inward (1). The arms begin to follow the breath and retract (2). Breathing outward, once again extension of the arms follows the breath (3). Breathing is from the hara, and therefore the hara always leads both movements. This should be studied carefully in Kokyu ho.

Reach out not only with your fingers and toes, but also with every part of your body and feeling, and draw ki to your center. When that ki reaches your one point, it establishes a complete circuit of ki, or spiritual energy. This is *kitai,* or your spiritual body. If you could peel back

■ *Fig. 3.2. Breath leads the body. Both retraction and expansion follow the breath from the hara.*

your skin, you would find bone. In the same way, if you could peel back the bone, you would find your kitai, or ki body. Simply keeping your ki extended by your concentration unites the center and periphery of your body. With time and practice this becomes automatic and requires no conscious effort.

■ Fig. 3.3. If you extend ki
at the moment of contact,
your partner should
rebound off your body.

Because of this your arms, although relaxed, do not collapse in spite of uke's pushing against your body. This is also true of your legs, neck, or any part of your body. When you are completely relaxed and centered, your ki becomes impenetrable. Merely opening your hands and extending ki at the moment of contact should cause your partner to rebound off your body, as if forcefully pushed.

The direction of your fingers should seek the path of least resistance in order to disperse the excessive energy of the collision. This dispersing of energy allows the body to move freely through the center of the technique. Do not try to move your fingers through your partner's resistance. The fingers should indicate the direction of the ki, yet it is the entire body as a unit that moves.

Because body movement is dictated by kokyu, the rhythm of breathing becomes the timing of the movement. Taking in your partner's ki, unify with his movement and let it determine your timing. Aikido is not an art of action-reaction. Practice *being,* rather than *doing*; *unifying with,* rather than *reacting to,* situations. The founder taught, *When my partner is slow, I am slow; when he is fast, I am fast.*

WHAT IS KI?

Japanese words used in the context of Aikido training are sometimes given mystical significance and other times simply left vague. As a result they are often misunderstood. The term *kokyu* was defined above, yet the ki, which we breathe and influence with our breath, needs to be demystified as well.

In meditation training, the development of ki is called *joriki,* or the power of concentration. In everyday spoken Japanese, *ki* generally refers to feeling or sensitivity. The expression for being alert, aware, or careful is *ki wo tsukeru,* "attach your ki." Another expression is *sonna ki ga suru,* which means, "I have a certain kind of feeling [about something]."

In a word, ki is *perception,* beginning with the level of feeling. In the Pali or Sanskrit tradition it is called *prana,* or *prajna,* which has the dual meaning of both "breath" and "wisdom." Ki is the energy that is always hidden yet ever present. It only appears as feeling and sensitivity, yet we are never apart from it. Without air we can survive for several minutes, yet without ki we would perish instantly.

Through the practice of kokyu, we come to realize that our spiritual body, or kitai, is much more substantial than the physical body, and more difficult to destroy. This creates an entirely different perspective on reality. We are not mainly physical beings, but rather beings of light and ki. It changes the way we feel and move, and also how we relate to our partner's body.

Through the practice of kokyu, ki can be developed to the point where it cannot be moved. Drawing in ki with the breath, it is possible to create a kind of spiritual skeleton that unifies the body. The human body is extremely fragile. Even the bones, which are the hardest and strongest part of the body, are broken quite easily. The ki is like a skeleton within the muscles and bones, yet it is more durable and longer lasting.

Aikido must be mind, or kokyu, over matter. This is not magic; it is nature's creative principle. Physical touch should be soft, yet the ki should be firm and strong, with no gaps. In order to develop this sensitivity, it is useful to become aware of the different dimensions of your ki, the kototama of A I E O U. When you practice in this way, Aikido becomes a tool for personal transformation rather than merely another martial art.

BUDDHIST VS. TAOIST BREATHING

The importance of developing ki for physical and spiritual power was understood long before the advent of Aikido. It was taught by Bodhidharma, the first ancestor of Zen Buddhism. Arriving from India at the Shaolin temple in China sometime between 55 and 75 CE, he saw that the monks were lacking in sufficient vitality to pursue their training with vigor. In order to remedy this situation, he created *chi kung*, a method of movement and breath coordination designed to strengthen the ki. This is believed to be the origin of the Chinese martial arts.

Training the body and the ki through the breath is expressed in many ancient proverbs, such as, *The superior man breathes from his heels.* And again, *The superior man breathes only once while crossing a long footbridge.* Bodhidharma came to the Shaolin temple to introduce the teachings of the Buddha, yet many of the monks were Taoists. The result was a blending of the Indian and the Chinese approaches to practice.

In meditation, the Buddhist method of *natural* breathing was used, yet in the physical practice of chi kung, the Taoist method of *reverse* breathing was employed. The Taoist method imitates the breathing of

■ *Fig. 3.4. Reverse breathing*

a newborn infant and makes it easier for the beginner to discover the breath-ki relationship.

In this practice the abdomen is drawn inward when breathing in and pushed outward when breathing out. Although this is in contrast to the more natural breathing of Aikido, it is useful as an intermediary stage in developing mental control of ki. This practice was also used to develop the legendary power of ki-ai, projecting ki outward with great force by shouting. It is said that the masters of olden times were able to bring down a bird in flight, or disarm an enemy, with a single shout.

BREATH AS SPIRITUAL PURIFICATION: THE FORMS OF MISOGI

Although many of the basic techniques of Aikido have their roots in older martial arts, some of the most important movements are derived from the misogi, or spiritual purification exercises of Japanese Shinto. These exercises are often used in warming up for practice, yet originally they were spiritual practices in and of themselves. The first of these are Funakogi and Furutama.

■ *Fig. 3.5. Funakogi, or boat rowing, generates ki.*

Funakogi and Furutama

Deguchi Onisaburo spoke of the significance of Funakogi in this way:

Within the great dryness of spiritual expanse, the mist of the ki of Su reaches outward infinitely. Extending both arms equally, the power of contrast (tata no chikara) is born. Both arms reach out as one yet contrast each other. This is the mind of makoto, extending through, and preserving, the infinite space of the universe. At this moment the six planes of meeting and the eight directions are established, and the power of contrast expands to its limits.

Funakogi, or boat rowing, imitates the motion of rowing a boat exactly. Standing in *hanmi* with the left foot forward, the hands are placed against the body so that they conform perfectly to the hips (1).

Remaining naturally balanced, the arms reach out and downward, sending ki out and down in front of the body. This movement is led with the index fingers and is accompanied by the ki-ai of IEt. (The final "t" sound stops the breath and holds the ki inside, which is necessary in correct ki-ai.) In order to finish in the proper position, both hands rotate inward as they extend (2).

Shifting the weight onto the back foot, rotate the arms outward, drawing in ki with the little fingers. The breath should be drawn up the spine as you imagine actually pulling something very heavy. This creates a kind of dynamic tension. Pulling back is accompanied by the ki-ai of Sa. Shifting to the opposite side with the right foot forward, the ki-ai becomes IEt and Ho (3).

The ki generated by Funakogi is then used to cleanse the blood moving to and from the hara and brain. This is done with the Furutama exercise. Standing with the feet approximately shoulder-width apart, raise your arms above your head until they meet. This is done with the in breath (1, 2, 3).

With the out breath, bring your hands down, left hand over the right in a cross, in front of your hara. The left side of the body is the more yang, or spiritual, side and should take the controlling position (4).

Keeping your weight on the balls of your feet, shake your hands and entire body as you send the breath and ki down to your hara. When the breath is exhausted, hold it momentarily as you continue shaking your hands. Gradually begin to use the breath to lead the ki up your spine until it fills your brain. Once again hold the breath, letting the ki sink into and cleanse the brain. This is the original meaning of "brainwashing."

As you begin to breathe out again, use your concentration to lead the ki down the front of your face and body until it again fills your hara. This may be repeated as many times as is comfortable, yet it is preferable to build the practice up gradually. If you continue this practice for up to ten to fifteen minutes, the entire body will become warm, even outdoors in winter.

Once again, the words of Deguchi Onisaburo:

Bring all the power of your being together, and shake your entire body while chanting the name of Ame no Minaka Nushi. In this way,

■ *Fig. 3.6. The Furutama exercise circulates the ki between the hara and the brain.*

strive to awaken to your true nature. This process must be repeated twice daily for several hours. Your food at this time should be one bowl of rice with umeboshi (pickled plum) and gomasio (sesame salt), twice daily. In this way you will return to the age of the gods.

Shin Kokyu: Deep Spiritual Breathing

After several cycles of Funakogi and Furutama, finish with *shin kokyu,* "deep spiritual breathing." This should begin with calming the mind and focusing only on one point. Your focus should be placed in your hara, which should be seen and felt as an empty vessel of ki.

It is no easy thing to actually bring your consciousness to reside in your hara; therefore, you should begin by using your breath to lead the ki to your one point. If you continue this practice in daily life as well as in on-the-mat training, eventually you will learn to use your intention to keep your mind in your one point.

Doing so is *chinkon kissin,* bringing the five senses to a relaxed and peaceful state and returning to the kototama of Su. Your body should be held upright by your breath and ki, not with the tension of physical muscle. Stand with your heels close together. This closes the anus and seals the ki in the body. Relaxing your shoulders, bring your ki from your one point to the crown of your head. With this feeling, reach your arms outward as if holding a large globe. This creates the heaven mudra, the kototama of AI.

Using the little fingers as a pivots, turn the palms upward. This expresses the kototama of A. The ki should be focused mainly in the little fingers. As you bring your breath and ki to your one point, expand the lower hara area.

"When speaking of expanding hara, this refers to the centripetal power which is at work at the same time that expansion occurs."[1] In other words, as your ki reaches your one point it is again brought down to the earth, and also up the spine to the crown chakra, and finally around to the third eye, or brow chakra.

Using your breath and concentration, draw ki upward from the earth and downward from the heavens. Your body rises up on the balls of your feet, and your head reaches upward toward Heaven (1).

■ Fig. 3.7. Shin kokyu: heaven mudra with the palms facing up expresses the kototama of A.

■ Fig. 3.8. Use the thumbs as a pivot point to arrive at the earth mudra, with palms facing down, expressing the kototama of OU.

As you begin to exhale, your body again sinks downward. Using your thumbs as a pivot point (2), turn the hands over and close the body. This creates the earth mudra and expresses the kototama of OU (3).

■ *Fig. 3.9. The cosmic mudra*

The heaven mudra is a more expanded version of the cosmic mudra used in Zen meditation. In Aikido it is used in many techniques for the practice of entering and unifying with your partner's ki. The rising of the fingers balances the sinking of the body, so that you are able to "ride" on top of your partner's center.

Your in breath always should be through your nose. The out breath may be through either the nose or the mouth, yet it should be slow, peaceful, and relatively silent in order to maintain the ki you have received with your inhalation.

FIRE, WATER, AND EARTH KI

The entire body should be held and controlled from one point, yet this is not possible for the beginner, or even for the intermediate Aikidoka. The place to begin, therefore, is with the *dotai*, the area reaching from the top of the diaphragm down to the legs. This is the source of the body's ki, and it should be kept open and unobstructed at all times.

The area in front of the dotai, or hara, is earth ki. It is the common space shared by you and your partner. It is where the activity of fire and water ki—the movement of the arms and hands—takes place. Movement of the arms always should be minimal in comparison to total body movement. In other words, the dotai moves first and is the source of your arm and leg movement. The simplest example is shown in the exercise called Kokyu undo.

■ *Fig. 3.10. Kokyu undo teaches the way of moving from the hara and changing from one hand form to another.*

Kokyu Undo

Sitting formally on your knees in the *seiza* posture, lean your body forward and physically transport your hara, first to the left and then to the right. This teaches the way of moving from the hara, rather than closing the dotai area and overextending the arms. Kokyu undo is not a stretching exercise. Rather it teaches the correct way of moving the body in general, and changing from one hand form to another in particular.

■ *Fig. 3.11. Handblade against a partner's body in* yokomen uchi, *a strike to the side of the head.*

Aikido Mudras: The Hand Forms of Aikido

The palm is the hara, or heart, of the hand. It is called *tanagokoro*. The thumb is the ruler of the fingers. It is also earth ki, the kototama of U dimension. It comfortably closes into the center of the palm. The palm should never be placed too firmly against your partner's body, as this cuts off the source of earth ki and makes unity impossible. In most cases, therefore, the handblade precedes the palm in making contact with uke's body.

The ki of the palm, when placed directly on your partner's body, should be given direction through the fingers rather than by pushing against your partner's body. The middle finger is the center of the center. Following the direction of this finger, go around direct contact with your partner's body, such as in this Kokyu osae movement.

Tanagokoro, the palm, is healing power, as opposed to the destroying power of the fist. When the hand is seen in this way, the palm is the healing ki of water, and the back of the hand is the destructive ki of fire. When closing the hand, place the bottom of the thumb against the upper inside of the index finger. This makes a complete circuit of earth ki. Closing the fist tightly stops the flow of your ki.

■ Fig. 3.12. Going around a partner's shoulder

■ Fig. 3.13. The fist mudra

■ Fig. 3.14. Atemi
from Tenchi nage:
rather than reaching
out to strike your
partner, let him run
into your atemi.

When striking, the fist may close still further, yet there should be space at the center at all times, and all tension should be released immediately following contact. In any case, the ideal strike in Aikido is the same feeling as that of Kokyu nage. As in Kokyu nage, it involves hara-to-hara, whole-body contact. It is more a matter of letting your partner run into your *atemi* (strike) than reaching out to strike. This can be seen in these *ryote tori* movements.

■ *Fig. 3.15.*
Handblade cutting
through uke's arm
defense

Rather than striking, however, the ki of fire is most commonly seen in the use of the handblade when cutting through uke's resistance. In this case, your concentration should be on cutting through uke's hara, rather than on moving his arm. If your feeling is correct, you can throw uke without moving his arm at all.

■ *Fig. 3.16. Kokyu nage from the elbow*

Water ki is used in pushing outward with the index finger side of the hand. This is seen when throwing Kokyu nage from uke's elbow, and also when bringing uke forward and down, and in the Yonkyo movement. If this is done with the palm, your ki will become over-extended.

■ *Fig. 3.17. Controlling the space in front of uke's dotai*

The proper use of earth ki is the control of space, especially the common space in front of your partner's dotai. Controlling this space is one way of exposing his vulnerability. Notice that the palm does not touch uke's arm in figure 3.17.

■ Fig. 3.18. Unobstructed earth ki in the palms allows you to control with the fire mudra and move to Ikkyo.

When placing your palm on your partner's arm or body, your hand should always rotate slightly, so that the palm touches only lightly and the main emphasis is on either the handblade side (fire) or on the index finger side (water).

Common to all of these forms is receiving uke's attack with your wrists, rather than your palms (1, 2). Receiving with your wrists, the earth ki of your palm is unobstructed and you are in position for grasping uke in a more useful manner. Controlling with the fire mudra, for example, you can pick up uke's elbow and move into Ikkyo (3, 4, 5).

Controlling with the earth mudra, you can easily apply a strike, or atemi, or change to the heaven mudra and lead your partner out into an Irimi nage technique (6, 7, 8).

■ *Fig. 3.19. Heaven mudra to Irimi nage*

■ Fig. 3.20. Using the water mudra to lead uke to the outside

■ Fig. 3.21. Here the water mudra forces uke's ki upward and inside.

Among the four basic hand forms of Aikido, the Heaven and Earth forms manifest the vertical ki of tate, sending the ki directly up and down. The fire and water forms also move vertically, yet they are used to send the ki out to the left and the right as well. In proper Aikido form, the turning of the body alone creates the horizontal movement.

When your arm is grasped on one side, step away from your partner and use the water mudra to lead uke to the outside of your body (1, 2).

As you move into his body with the water mudra, draw the ki up your spine and send uke's ki upward and to the inside (3).

■ *Fig. 3.22. Using the fire mudra to bring uke down and to the inside*

As you move away from your partner with the fire mudra, he is brought both down and to the inside (4).

Leading your partner's ki upward with water mudra is common to all basic Kokyu nage techniques and should be carefully studied (5, 6, 7). There is no lifting with your arm. Rather, draw the ki up your spine, even as you extend your fingers; the only lifting is done with your hara. The subtle balance of drawing ki inward while extending creates a wave pattern—an essential point of kokyu training.

■ *Fig. 3.23. One-handed Tenchi nage: leading uke's ki upward with the water mudra*

Iki:
The Breath of Life

■ *Fig. 3.24. The mind leads the breath, the wrists, and the fingers from heaven mudra into fire mudra.*

The breath always leads the physical movement of the body. Changing from the heaven form (1) to the fire form, place your thumbs in a straight line with your wrists (2) and rotate the fingers around the thumbs until they rise up into fire mudra (3). The mind leads the breath as you breathe inward (fire), drawing first the wrists and then the fingers upward into fire mudra.

■ Fig. 3.25. Changing from fire mudra to water mudra and back to earth mudra

To move from fire mudra to water mudra, use the little fingers as pivot points and turn your hands outward until the thumbs are exactly on top (4, 5). From water mudra, change back into earth mudra by using the thumbs as pivot points (6). In this way, the mind leads the breath, the breath leads the ki, and the ki leads the body. Changing among these four basic forms, all the hand movements of Aikido emerge naturally.

呼 吸 法

KOKYU HO

Kokyu ho, the method of kokyu, is the first partner practice in Aikido. In its original form it was called Reiki ho, or the training method for developing spiritual ki. Setting the stage for all Aikido practice, it is an intuitive method of discovery—the proper way of focusing the ki to accomplish whole body and mind unification.

As shown in the section on the eight powers, visible movement is born with the power of contrast, the advent of A dimension's ki. This visible expansion, however, should be rooted in I dimension's ki, your one point. Every aspect of movement must always be balanced by the opposite direction of force, or ki. With your first in breath, draw straight lines of ki into your one point from all directions. As mentioned in chapter 2, these straight lines of ki should run through and support the cursive form of your arms. You should endeavor to blend the movement of your physical body with these straight lines of ki. In this way your forward energy, the ki of tate, will always be stronger than the ki of yoko.

■ *Fig. 3.26. The straight lines of ki (I) enter our one point from all directions, and support the cursive form (E) of the arms.*

Reaching upward, manifest *ten no kokyu*, "the breath of Heaven" (1). Draw breath and ki down to tanden no ichi, the one point at the center of your hara. This is to bring *hi no ki*, the in breath of *izanagi*, into your own hara and union with the earth. As your body opens (A), you draw breath inward, stabilizing your center (I).

■ *Fig. 3.27. Ten no kokyu: the breath of Heaven*

■ Fig. 3.29. Chi no kokyu: the breath of Earth

■ Fig. 3.30. Hanmi handachi: grab his hips and throw.

■ Fig. 3.31. Mizu no te begins Kokyu ho: establish the vertical connection between uke and nage.

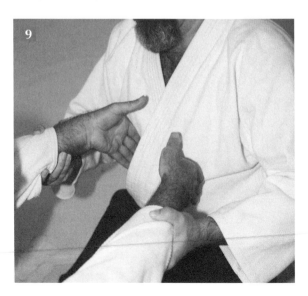

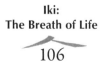

This is the kototama of AI. In the time it takes to open your hands and draw in breath, your entire body should be filled with and unified by ki. As you draw this ki down to your center, give it direction with your fingers. From your one point, the straight lines of ki reaching out in all directions create the power of contrast (Ta). (See 2, 3, and 4 on page 105.) This is *kokyu ryoku,* or the power of kokyu. It is the result of pushing on your own center rather than pushing against your partner's power.

Before you can move another person, you must be able to receive power in the earth and unify with it. Feel the emptiness of your physical body. This is U dimension's ki. At the center of hara is Wi, the wellspring of life power. Place your thumb against your middle finger, connecting the kototama of U and I, and breathe inward. This manifests *chi no kokyu,* "the breath of Earth" (5, 6).

Practicing with a partner, this same kokyu is used to draw his ki into your hara, and then down even further into the earth. Uke will find himself pushing vertically down on the earth, rather than horizontally into your power (7). Extending your ki and unifying with his power, you will be able to move him at will (8).

With your first inhalation (Yi), the life will (I) and power (Wi) are united. To bring these two together in your one point is to stand in the center and unify the ki of fire and water. When you can really do this, you will be able to destroy the mind of conflict before it can even manifest.

Sitting in the formal position of seiza, your knees and those of your standing partner form a square. The ki of your left hip should cut diagonally through the square and enter directly into the ki of your partner's left hip.

The first relationship to consider in Aikido is always the vertical connection between uke and nage (9). When your wrists are grasped, you should thrust straight forward into uke's center with the water mudra. Drawing breath inward and up your spine will cause uke's ki to rise upward, allowing your hands to gradually shift into fire mudra.

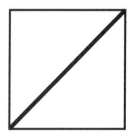

■ *Fig. 3.28. Square becomes two triangles.*

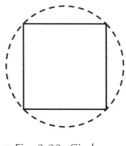

■ Fig. 3.32. Kokyu ho: moving through uke's resistance is circular.

■ Fig. 3.33. Circle over square

■ Fig. 3.34. The pelvic cage forms an incomplete circle.

The vertical unity you've established with uke should be maintained and distributed horizontally as you move through the technique. Moving through uke's resistance is circular. In order to see this clearly, connect the four corners of the square with a circle. This is the pattern your body will follow as you move through uke's resistance.

When your hips meet those of your partner, the focus of your ki should be on entering your partner's hips diagonally and passing through his one point to exit on the opposite side. In order to see this more clearly, observe the shape of the pelvic cage. Seen from above it is an incomplete circle.

If the circle were to be completed, your one point would become the center of that circle and the most forward part of the circle becomes the common space you share with your partner (see fig. 3.35). The one who controls this common space controls the situation.

It is a very subtle point to grasp the correct feeling for the turning of your upper body as your hips pass energetically through those of your partner. First of all, your hara-to-hara focus should send uke's ki upward, thereby unbalancing him. If there is any sharp or forceful turning of the hips, your power will remain on the outside of uke's body and unification will be lost.

In ryote tori techniques, the right and left arms often appear to have the same function. One side, however, is fire ki, and the other is water. Fire ki leads the movement and draws uke's ki out of his body. If this is mistaken there will be a collision of force. Do not attempt to lift your arms. The hands should feel as if they are moving independently from the body. There should be almost no physical feeling between the hips and the wrists, as if the hands and hips are connected by ki alone. To the degree that uke's balance is uprooted by your whole body contact, your arms will rise up naturally.

The direction of your fingertips gives the energy of the collision an avenue of escape, which, in turn, allows movement to continue. Case by case, the direction of your fingertips will differ depending on the manner in which uke grasps your arms. If uke is grasping from above, you bring him up still further.

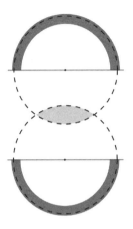

■ *Fig. 3.35. Two circles connecting common space*

■ *Fig. 3.36. Kokyu ho: when uke grasps from above, bring him higher.*

Fig. 3.37. Kokyu ho: when uke grasps from below, bring him down.

If he grasps from below, bring him down.

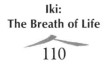

KOKYU NAGE

There seems to be endless variety in the Kokyu nage techniques of Aikido, yet all of these techniques, upon closer inspection, will be seen to follow the same principle and basic form. As kokyu techniques they are based on the threefold principle of receiving, carrying, and releasing ki and manifesting the basic form of Kokyu ho.

The final stage of releasing, however, is somewhat different from what the term *nage* implies. In Aikido, uke falls mainly due to losing his balance, or what is called *kuzushi*. Your arms rest on uke's body and ride upward like an ocean wave hitting a rock in the sea. Never push down on uke's body. Although your ki thrusts directly into uke's hara, your weight should sink down into the earth, directly where you stand.

When you ride on uke's center in this way, his reaction is to push upward to protect himself from a possible strike. When uke reacts by pushing upward, receive his power in your one point and unify with it. This being accomplished, he will be unbalanced easily.

Since Aikido is a noncompetitive martial art, it requires a serious attitude regarding protecting oneself from danger. In the words of O-sensei: *One blow in Aikido is capable of killing an opponent. In practice, obey your instructor, and do not make the practice period a time for needless testing of strength. There is no place for ego in Aikido practice.*

At least in theory, there are no limitations on the possible strikes, or even lethal techniques, that could be applied. In some cases, therefore, uke will intentionally take a fall in order to avoid the possibility of being hit. This develops the proper awareness for actual self-defense.

Sometimes the term Kokyu nage is translated as "rhythm throw." It is like a wave of energy through which you communicate with your partner. When uke lunges forward to grasp your wrists, he is breathing outward. Extending your arms, you breathe inward and in this way harmonize with his kokyu and intention. In the case of an experienced practitioner, this can happen even before physical contact is made.

As a result, uke's power returns to him at the moment of contact. The first movement of your partner, therefore, is already your second movement, the first being accomplished by mind and breath alone. When practiced in this way, in response to either a grasping or a punching attack, the attitude is the same. Let us look at some specific examples.

Tenchi Kokyu Nage

Tenchi nage, the Heaven-Earth throw, is not usually considered as a Kokyu nage, yet it is the most natural next step from Kokyu ho. As in all Aikido techniques, hara initiates the movement, the ki of which is then transferred to the wrists. The fingertips arrive at their final position last. In this way, the upper hand (fire) begins in the water mudra and draws uke's ki up and outward. If it changes into fire mudra too soon, the technique will fail. The lower hand (water) sends ki centripetally into uke's hara (1). Together they create the form of the movement.

The subtle reality is, once again, concealed in the relationship between the upper and lower body. When your hips move backward your arms extend (tate). As your body rises, your hips turn in the opposite direction from the movement of your arms (yoko) (2, 3). This exemplifies the principle of balance in the eight powers. As a result, the degree or intensity of your physical contact with uke remains unchanged, and the ki of tate remains dominant over that of yoko throughout the movement. There is no pushing or pulling, only expansion and contraction of your body. This movement is what creates the undulation or wave pattern in Aikido techniques. If hands and hips move together in the same direction, your are still using force against force.

When your two hands are grasped, it seems that you can't move, yet your hips are free. By balancing tate and yoko, as described above, your arms appear to move while the hips remain stationary. In reality, however, it is only the hara that actually initiates and maintains the movement (4, 5). Uke's ki is led out of his body and he is drawn forward as if into a vacuum. Because you do not push on your partner, he cannot use your power to his advantage. Because you do not pull on him, he can't let go without the danger of being hit. In this way, Aikido techniques strive to establish a constant unification with your partner as you move through the technique.

The footwork of Tenchi nage is exemplary of Aikido footwork in general. The technique is accomplished in three steps, yet they blend together in such a way as to appear to be only two. Stepping back with the right foot as your arms extend, you then shift your weight to the left leg, allowing it to become a pivot point for the right leg to move forward again. In this way, there appear to be only two actual steps.

This shifting of the weight from one side to the other is the correct way of moving in Aikido. The only time your weight should be on both feet is when they are placed close enough together. Your movement should be like a large tree being blown around in a storm. In this way, learn to use hara for power rather than your shoulders. This way of moving should be practiced when doing *ukemi* as well.

Finally, in Tenchi nage as well as Irimi nage, the final release or throw should not be attempted by pushing horizontally against uke. A

■ *Fig. 3.38. Tenchi kokyu nage: the hips move backward as the arms extend, drawing uke forward as if into a vacuum.*

■ Fig. 3.39. The final throw should not be attempted by pushing horizontally.

■ Fig. 3.40. The kotai form of Tenchi nage with the elbow placed under uke's chin

■ Fig. 3.41. Move diagonally into uke's body for the throw.

moment of reflection should reveal that horizontal confrontation could be successful only with brute force.

Drawing uke's ki inward with the hand of fire, turn his head backward. In the kotai form of Tenchi nage, the elbow is actually placed under uke's chin to tip his head backward. Uke will be turned over and easily thrown straight down toward the mat. In other words, your throwing arm should be inverted, rather than extended, when throwing.

When throwing, move diagonally into uke's body.

■ Fig. 3.42. Katate tori kokyu nage: to avoid uke's free hand or a kick, step behind his forward foot.

■ Fig. 3.43. Receive uke with the water mudra to send ki upward.

Katate Tori Kokyu Nage

Doing techniques from *katate tori,* a one-hand grasp, is one of the most basic training methods in Aikido. It's common to question why anyone would grasp with katate tori, yet the trained martial artist can bring a man down with this kind of grasp. The immediate danger in katate tori, however, is from uke's free hand or a kick. In order to avoid this, step behind uke's forward foot in such a way as to turn his body away from you.

It has been said that this kind of technique might be ineffective because the person being thrown would release his grasp. This is a misconception. If your ki is always going into uke's weak point, he cannot release his grasp without becoming vulnerable to a strike.

When uke grasps your wrist, the path of least resistance should determine the direction of your fingers. Regardless of the degree of uke's power, your hand is on the other side of his grasp and your fingers are able to move freely. In order to enter directly into his hara, and also send his ki upward, receive with the water mudra. If you receive properly, you will hold uke with your hara, even as he holds your arm.

■ *Fig. 3.44. Tate-yoko:
your ki should enter
below uke's hara and rise
as a vertical spiral.*

Your ki should enter below uke's hara and continue to rise up from
beneath his power. If this feeling is understood, you will avoid a collision of power. This clearly illustrates the first tate-yoko relationship of
Aikido movement—that of a vertically rising spiral.

Leading uke's energy out of his body with your arms, while sending
the ki of your hara directly into his hara, establishes the triangle principle. As a result, uke will find himself unable to discover the source
of the power that moves him, and your own arms will be able to move
freely. As you seem to meet uke's force directly, your hands and hips
move in opposite directions. This keeps the focus of your hara entering
directly into uke's hara, rather than following his arms, which would
cause you to become overextended.

Moving forward, the hands resemble thrusting with a sword or
spear. As with a spear, the hand that is closer to your hara provides the
power for the thrust. Even though this hand has no physical contact,
it carries the power of the hara. Practicing with this kind of concentration utilizes whole body movement and, once again, helps avoid the
problem of overextending your arms.

In the kotai form, nage enters into uke's diagonal and threatens an
elbow atemi.

When the feeling of whole body unity has been mastered, however,
it is possible to thrust straight forward and cause uke's body to turn
away from you.

■ Fig. 3.45. Thrusting as with a spear

■ Fig. 3.46. The kotai form threatens uke with an elbow atemi.

■ Fig. 3.47. With whole body unity, a straight thrust can turn uke's body away from you.

■ Fig. 3.48. When throwing, do not turn back toward uke as shown here.

Just as in thrusting with a spear, the forward hand turns inward toward the center of the movement. The turning of the arms is a horizontal movement (yoko) and should remain secondary to the forward thrust (tate). Do not attempt to turn back toward uke when throwing. Continue your forward direction until uke is unbalanced.

■ *Fig. 3.49. Correct form for the katate tori throw; the body continues to turn away from uke*

The movement of throwing resembles withdrawing a spear after thrusting. Your body continues to pass through the movement without turning back (1). As you throw, your upper hand turns outward, opening the body (2). This is the opening and closing of your kokyu.

Ryote Tori Kokyu Nage

When your partner grasps both of your hands, it is usually to set you up for a forward kick or head butt. The simplest way to deal with this is to bring him down with the heaven mudra. Let the direction of your ki go around his arms (tate) rather than pushing down on them (3, 4). If you push down, he will escape and strike you (5).

■ Fig. 3.50. Bring uke
down with the heaven
mudra, rather than trying
to push his arms down.

■ Fig. 3.51. Bringing uke down with one arm and atemi

■ Fig. 3.52. Throwing uke with a Kaiten nage move

If there is time, step back diagonally and bring uke down with one arm (1) and strike atemi (2).

If uke ducks to the outside of your atemi and attempts to tackle your legs (3), maintain a wide hanmi (4) and throw with a Kaiten nage movement (5).

■ *Fig. 3.53. Basic techniques* (kihon waza) *of Ryote tori kokyu nage*

For the most basic Ryote tori kokyu nage technique, enter into uke's power with the water mudra (6) and bring him down with the form of fire (7). As you step back, your outside arm becomes fire ki and leads uke's ki out of his body. If you draw his body in properly, his ki will rise upward and become unstable (8).

■ *Fig. 3.54. Ryote tori kokyu nage: attempting to throw uke downward allows him to push you from behind.*

Understanding Kokyu nage, or any of the techniques of Aikido, requires a very practical attitude. If you ignore the proper focus and attempt to throw uke downward, he will easily release his grasp and push you from behind (1, 2). Contrary to common perception, throwing is never downward.

Sinking your body and pushing diagonally into uke is a preparation for defense (3, 4). This is also preparation for a body block or strike. Throwing properly is like cracking a whip; the dynamic result is at the very end, not at the moment of reaching outward. The arms may appear to throw by moving outward, but this is not the case. Throwing in every case is the result of releasing tension and allowing the arms to pull back toward your body (5). The actual throwing motion is upward.

■ *Fig. 3.55. Ryote tori kokyu nage: sinking your weight and releasing tension is the correct technique for throwing uke.*

Morote Tori Kokyu Nage

Another important Kokyu nage is from the morote tori attack, with your partner's two hands grasping one of your arms. This kind of attack is used to apply the Yonkyo control that will be discussed in chapter 4. It is also used to hold one side of your body when several people attack you. The latter case will be dealt with below.

When uke grasps with morote tori, unbalance him with mizu no te and strike atemi with hi no te (1). Your grasped arm sends ki upward with the fire mudra, thereby balancing the downward sinking of your hara. Once again, this is the outward, or visible, form. The feeling of your ki is that your hips move in the opposite direction of your grasped arm.

In order to avoid your atemi, uke may try to move behind you. In this case, bend your body forward and turn away from him (2). The back of your hand should be turned toward your body and the ki of your fingers extended so that you can move uke with your hara (3), rather than trying to pull him with your arm. Your arm should rest lightly against your body as if holding a fragile object under it.

Leading the movement with your free hand, move your body in an expanding spiral (4). The feeling should be that of escaping from uke's grasp, rather than trying to pull him with you. If you pull on uke, as with a rope, he will easily stop your movement. Keep your arms bent and extend ki with your fingers. Uke must be led by your hara-to-hara ki connection.

As uke comes around, lead your hand forward with the water mudra (5), gradually raising your fingers into fire mudra. It is impossible to raise his arm with your own. Rather, receive the power of his resistance in your hara and use it to move your own arm for the throw (6).

The final form of throwing is the same as that used in the Katate tori kokyu nage technique, or it may be the form of drawing a sword and cutting diagonally downward (7).

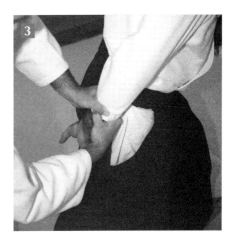

■ Fig. 3.56. Defending against a morote tori attack with Morote tori kokyu nage

■ *Fig. 3.57. Defending against a morote tori attack by two people*

Finally, as mentioned above, if two people restrain you (1), the following variation is appropriate. Choose the side of the stronger opponent and move into him as in a Katate tori shiho nage technique (2). Stepping through, draw the other opponent into your raised arm, like threading a needle (3). Entering deeply with irimi, throw both opponents simultaneously (4).

■ *Fig. 3.58. Defending against an ushiro attack with kubi shime, a choke hold*

Ushiro Kokyu Nage

The number of possible Kokyu nage techniques in Aikido is almost endless, yet the student who grasps the basic principles described above may go on to apply these ideas in other places. The discussion of Kokyu nage would, however, be incomplete without considering *ushiro* attacks, or being grasped from behind.

In the ushiro attack it is often appropriate to keep the front of the body concave and sink the shoulders. Attempting to keep the body rigidly vertical is common in Aikido, and it leads to a very limited exploration of technique. The body should always be firmly rooted in hara yet able to bend in all directions freely.

Kubi Shime

The ushiro attack is often an attempt to pull you backward or to choke from behind. If your body is flexible, you can bend with this kind of movement and use it to your advantage.

■ *Fig. 3.59. Techniques for defending against an ushiro ryote tori attack*

Ryote Tori

When both of your wrists are grasped from behind, drop all tension and sink into uke's hara. Let your breath, or ki power alone, make your body impenetrable to uke's attack (1).

A common defense against the ushiro ryote tori attack is to attempt an elbow strike. If uke blocks this atemi, his grasp can be used to throw him (2, 3).

If, however, you hold your palms upward too long, uke will grasp your body and restrain your elbows. Extend your arms outward with the feeling of extension, rather than lifting, and raise your hara upward to fill the void of his grasp. From this position you can thrown him as if sliding him off the side of a wall (4, 5).

In the standard Ushiro ryote tori kokyu nage, your arms should be

raised from your hara in such a way as to cause uke's entire body weight to ride on top of them, yet there should be no tension in your shoulders. Lifting is done with your hara alone (6), never with the arms. Throwing here, as in many Aikido techniques, is a matter of changing places with your partner. If the function of your arms takes place in the comfortable space in front of your body, uke will be unable to release his grasp. If, on the other hand, you overextend your arms, uke will pull you over easily or release his grasp and push you forward.

As in the morote tori example above, sinking the body is a preparation for throwing. If you remove your own body, leaving uke nothing to push down on, he will lose balance. This is most obvious if you throw by sitting down and allowing uke to fly over you. The final coup de grace is lifting with your arms to give uke added momentum (7, 8, 9).

4 ■ SHUGYO

The Spiritual Training of Technique

■ *Shugyo*

THE RANKING SYSTEM OF AIKIDO

Traditional ranking in the Japanese martial arts was divided into three levels: *shoden, chuden,* and *okuden. Sho* means "beginning," *chu* means "intermediate," and o*ku* means the "depths," or advanced. *Den* means "to pass down." In other words, a person's level depended solely on the actual ability acquired. As you might be called upon to defend yourself, proclaiming a title beyond your actual ability could end in extreme embarrassment, or even death.

The idea of the dan system seems to have originated in China, yet it can be roughly superimposed over the idea of these three levels. From that perspective, shoden, the beginning level, may be seen as *shodan, nidan,* and *sandan.* The middle level of chuden would be *yondan, godan,* and *rokudan*—fourth, fifth, and sixth dan. The level of mastery would begin from seventh (*nana*) dan and be complete at ninth dan. Tenth dan has no place in this system. The number ten, written with a cross, is a symbol of God or perfection.

The physical practice of Aikido is a tool that we use to discover the principles of movement underlying both body and mind. It is to be approached as in the Japanese proverb, *ishi no ue ni san nen,* or three

■ *Ishi no ue ni sannen*

130

years sitting on a rock. This means you must devote yourself single-mindedly, without the slightest deviation, for at least three years in order to become shodan—a beginner.

Shodan, in Aikido, implies that the form of basic technique, or kotai training, has been understood. At the nidan level the Aikidoka should be fluent in these forms and able to perform them naturally and quickly. It is not advisable to concentrate too much on power at this point. If the Aikidoka becomes locked into form at this level, it can destroy the fluidity necessary for higher development.

Sandan (third level) is mastery of shoden and the beginning of ryutai training. Power is added to fluidity. It is a kind of *shinshin toitsu,* or body and ki unification. It is sometimes said to be the time of the greatest physical power, yet stagnation is also a real danger here. If power and technique are mistaken for mastery, further progress is impossible.

At the level of sandan, one should reflect on the balance of will (fire) and vitality (water). When vitality is held in tow by will, there will be harmony. When vitality is stronger than will, however, it leads to chaos. Learning to balance these two and bring them into harmony leads to the wisdom of self-knowledge.

Yondan begins chuden training; the fusion of body and ki achieved at the sandan level must be untied in order to discover greater freedom and control. Each part of the body should be able to move independently, yet without losing whole body unity. In other words, the direction of physical movement doesn't necessarily indicate the direction in which one's ki is focused.

At the yondan level, the intuitive study of the eight powers as yin and yang begins. Dropping the physical power of sandan, hands and hips are set free and become able to move in a complementary fashion, independent of each other. There is a constant shift in concentration between form and feeling. Form should be given first importance until unification with your partner is achieved. At that moment, feeling becomes more important.

Godan (fifth dan) is the pivotal point in the study of Aikido. Five, halfway between one and nine, indicates the vertical ki of I dimension, the fulcrum of principle. Placing the mind in one point is the beginning of the training, yet at fifth dan, one point should be grasped as the pivotal point for yin and yang, the control center for the entire body.

Traditionally fifth dan was the first level at which it was considered respectable to teach others. At this level the Aikidoka should be able to discover and correct his or her own mistakes. This is not possible without a humble and unassuming attitude. In other words, he or she should be able, if necessary, to continue to grow in a healthy and correct direction even without a teacher.

At sixth dan your spiritual constitution should be established. This means that your ki has become yang, or positive. At this level your kitai, or ki body, is understood as the fundamental reality. Great power is there, but always in reserve. On the outside one's feeling is gentle. This is *mono ni narimashita,* or to become accomplished.

Seventh dan is the first level of mastery. The focus is no longer technique, but rather complete freedom in manifesting Aikido principle. At this stage the Aikidoka should be able to control his or her ki by intention alone. The reality is that no one has any more ki than anyone else; it is how we use our mind in directing our ki that really matters. This is the beginning of real spiritual training; there should be no anger or attachment to winning.

The eighth and ninth dan levels are mainly concerned with the application of one's understanding to all aspects of life. The single most important thing for the study of Aikido, regardless of rank, is a continual spirit of research. Without this, one can hardly be called a master.

Beginning with shodan, it is important to grasp the meaning of each level so that the student is aware of the next step in training. It is also valuable to create consistency in the ranks of students around the world. Without this, the entire system loses its meaning.

There has been a tendency in the West to use rank as a means of organization building. This is irresponsible and harmful to the system, as well as to the individual students. If rank is given too early, there is a strong tendency for the student to lose direction and stagnate.

THE LEVELS OF TRAINING

Although Aikido is strongly influenced by both Japanese swordsmanship and jujutsu, its spiritual principle derives solely from the kototama principle as taught by Deguchi Onisaburo. O-sensei was known to lecture on these teachings from time to time at the Byakko, or "white light" organization in Tokyo. He described Aikido by saying, *Aikido is one spirit, four souls, three origins, and eight powers.*

In chapter 1, the three levels called *kanagi, sugaso,* and *futonorito* were introduced. One spirit and four souls were also explained as the vowel dimensions. In our physical training these should be understood as: A = expansion, the life of the technique; O = contraction and continuity; U = hara, the source of our ki; E = the direction of our ki; and I = one point, the source of our movement.

The continually expanding feeling of A dimension should be maintained at all times. Without it our technique reverts back to brute force. O dimension's ki creates natural weight and concentration, the source of our power. E dimension's ki gives direction to that power, and I dimension's ki roots it in our center.

O-sensei also utilized the teaching of kanagi, sugaso, and futonorito to explain the stages of Aikido development and training. These are kotai (solid), jutai (flexible), and ryutai (flowing), with each level depending on mastery of the preceding one. Ryutai is already mastery, yet at a later date the fourth level of kitai, the technique of mind over matter, was added. Let us look at how these levels work in the progress of Aikido.

Kanagi (Kotai Training)

The kanagi, or physical, approach is based on the physical perspective of U dimension's ki, yet it eventually reveals our ki body as well. Our ki is like a coat rack on which the physical body hangs. This way of practice is called *kotai,* or solid body training.

With this approach you can't see the expansive quality of A dimension's ki, yet kotai training develops our sense of touch and centers us in one point. In Japanese Budo, therefore, the training of *sumo,* based on *tai-atari,* or a direct collision of force, was originally practiced by all male children. Without this kind of training, the ability to unify with your partner's ki on a deeper level will be very difficult to discover. Those who would shy away from direct physical contact in the beginning rarely discover the power of unification upon which Aikido depends.

Kotai training is the foundation of our physical awareness, our sense of touch. The skin is the original brain; the sense of touch, therefore, is the foundation of intuitive perception. In either spiritual or physical training, the first important awareness that must be developed is awareness of the body.

The very real difficulty of moving when you are grasped firmly offers an opportunity to change your focus from physical muscle to technique. In this way the intricate details of technique are grasped one by one.

It is within a situation of direct conflict, where physical muscle no longer works, that the triangle principle, the foundation of all basic techniques, is first encountered. Kotai training also applies to basic movement, or block-letters training, in which the student moves through the triangle pattern of the technique. Using this form, a direct confrontation of physical muscle can be used to discover the basic method of unbalancing a partner.

This is also what O-sensei called Aratama training. The emphasis here is on developing physical power and durability of the bones and muscles, yet it should not be at the expense of flexibility. The natural progression of development is from the flexible to the solid.

The earth, for example, was born from a gaseous state that later materialized into water, and finally into the firmness of land. Even our bones are still very flexible at birth. Progress comes abruptly to a halt once a fixed form is accomplished. Proper Aikido training, therefore, should begin with large, free, and flexible movements.

A tight muscle cannot be made stronger. There is no value, at any time, in practicing with stiff muscles. You should approach basic training with whole body and mind contact, yet the muscles, especially the shoulders, should never be stiff. Studying tai-atari, or whole body contact, seeks the method of moving beyond a direct collision of power.

Sugaso

In contrast to the physical order of kanagi, the sugaso order (AOUE) is a more spiritual approach to training. It is based on the continued expansion of A dimension's ki. This is AO, the training of Sakitama and Nigitama. A dimension's ki creates the all-embracing attitude necessary for relaxed practice. O dimension gives it continuity as *ki-musubi,* or tying your ki together with that of your partner. As A dimension's ki matures, it comes forth as O. Attachment diminishes and harmony replaces competition as a tool for the mutual success of both your partner and yourself.

The water ki of AO manifests the jutai, or flexible body approach to Aikido technique. This is the next natural step from kotai training. In addition to developing flexibility and effortless power, it also nurtures the maturity of the highest human qualities—a sense of caring for and nurturing others. It instills a sense of orderliness in bringing things to fruition.

The training of Nigitama is the development of ki and the ability to project it outward. This is impossible until all the tension is removed from the shoulders. Master Koichi Tohei once stated, "There is space between skin and bone." In other words, there is always room to move if you are flexible.

At first this approach may seem counterproductive, because power is not immediately forthcoming. In the long run, however, the much greater power of ki will be discovered. In the sugaso approach to Aikido techniques, all defensiveness must be thrown away. This is the spirit of all-embracing acceptance. As you continually open the body, the arms cease to be an obstruction between uke and you.

As a learning method, sugaso teaches waiting and fully receiving your partner's power before attempting to throw. Until this is understood, Aikido technique is not effective as either self-defense or spiritual training. Resisting the urge to throw, you realize that there is plenty of time.

Maintaining unity in movement is ki-musubi, the uniqueness of Aikido training. In this way you manifest *inori,* or prayer. It is blending your ki with that of your partner and riding on his center. In Aikido we should attempt to control from above, rather than opposing each other on a horizontal plane.

The sugaso approach is also not reliable for self-defense until mastery of the ryutai form has been achieved; it tends to leave the beginner overly vulnerable. In his later years, however, O-sensei preferred to emphasize the beauty and spiritual feeling of Aikido through this approach. He used this kind of movement in his public demonstrations, precisely, it would seem, to show that expansive and graceful movement actually can be effective.

Futonorito

The futonorito approach expresses the integration of the physical and the spiritual. It is the middle way, the way of standing in the center. This is based on the kototama of IE, the expression of supreme wisdom. This order manifests itself as ryutai techniques. Once again, this is the training of Kushitama (I) and Aratama (E).

With the futonorito order (AIEOU), the expansion of A dimension is instantaneously anchored in I dimension, our one point. This is AI, the harmony from which proper movement should begin. With the expansion of A rooted in I dimension, it is then given an economical and precise direction by the judgment of E. The balance between the three kototama of AIE is the mark of a master. It is the highest order of both body and mind.

The emphasis here is on the continual development of greater precision, subtlety, and sensitivity. As judgment (and therefore movement) becomes more refined, sensitivity to I dimension, the function of one point, is increased. When one point becomes the source of your movement, Aikido becomes "moving Zen."

Practicing the futonorito order of movement mimics the movement of nature and thereby develops economy and precision of movement. The unification of Heaven (A) and Earth (I) is like the sun melting the ice of winter and giving freedom to the streams and tributaries, which, seeking the path of least resistance (E), run out to the ocean. The oceans are filled and tie together (O) the landmass (U).

Based on the futonorito order, ryutai training is immediately both practical and spiritual. In ryutai training there is no separation between offense and defense. The moment your partner is set on his movement, you already should be leading his ki with your hara. Practicing *sente,* or initiative, you move at the same time as your partner.

In other words, you must be able to make an immediate mental connection between uke's hara and your own. If you attempt to lead his ki without this kind of mental focus, he will use your movement against you. If you maintain this awareness, uke will be unable to withdraw his original intention.

In ryutai techniques, all of the basic points of kotai are abbreviated, but never omitted. The three-step process of entering, performing the technique, and throwing must happen in one movement. The form becomes ultimately simple, yet immediately effective. This is possible depending on an increasing degree of faith in one's own center.

Through ryutai training, E dimension's ki matures, bringing precision, grace, and skill into your movement. Dependency on forcefulness and manipulation is replaced by trust and faith in your own being. I dimension's ki can be reached only by the continually sagacious perception of E dimension's ki. These two are so tied together that it is impossible to train one without the other.

As the most immediately practical and realistic, ryutai, the training of E dimension's ki, should be the main emphasis in our daily training. Kotai and jutai may be used to emphasize particular points on a case-by-case basis. For the advanced student, the emphasis can occasionally be shifted from ryutai (E) to kitai (I) techniques. This is the development of spirit, or mind, over matter. It requires the ability to direct your ki instantaneously wherever it is needed, and to create subtle changes in a given situation merely by adjusting the focus of your one point.

In kitai techniques there may or may not be any physical connection at all, yet if uke is able to establish contact, he should immediately be thrown by that contact. In other words, your ki must be connected as strongly as if there were a physical connection.

BODY MOVEMENT

In O-sensei's five rules of Aikido we find, *Daily practice begins with light movements of the body, gradually increasing in intensity and strength, but there must be no overexertion. That is why even an elderly person can continue to practice with pleasure and without bodily harm, and why he will attain the goal of his training. Do not contradict nature; moderation is the key.*

This relaxed approach begins even before movement. The vowel dimensions should be brought into our practice by studying the way of holding our body, the way of touch, and the direction and unification of our ki. It begins with our stance, the way we hold our body and mind.

■ *Fig. 4.1. Proper hanmi stance forms a straight line between ear and knee.*

The real stance of Aikido is *shizentai* or *mugamae,* a natural standing posture. When we step forward into the triangle, or hanmi stance, this relaxed state must continue. Practicing with a low stance helps to develop the hips and legs, the source of your power.

"The position of the center of gravity of the body as an object is a little above the exact middle of the height of the body. In Budo, it is the knees that play the role of adjusting this difference. By bending the knees slightly and lowering the center of gravity, the center of gravity and the center of the body are unified."[1]

In the Chinese martial arts this is called the "mountain-climbing stance." Your feeling should remain open. The feeling of defense invites offense, while a positive and open stance is ready, alert, and difficult to penetrate. Being relaxed yet aware leaves you best able to deal with whatever happens.

Attempting to be too vertical creates tension in the lower back and makes relaxed power difficult. Practicing in this way for too long may even cause injury to the lower back area. The body should be held upright by the breath and from one point. When the mind is firmly centered in one point, posture automatically becomes upright.

In a proper hanmi stance there should be a straight line from your

■ *Fig. 4.2. The posture of
gratitude*

ear to your shoulder, and all the way down to your knee. In this way
there will be no tension in the lower back.

Once you understand the correct feeling in your stance, the next
step is to practice ki extension. Standing in hanmi, this becomes the
posture of gratitude. Breathing the ki of the atmosphere (Heaven) and
Earth into your one point, extend your fingers and send it out again,
giving back to nature and the universe.

Each joint controls the joint above, yet it is the breath, or ki, running through the joints that makes them functional. When uke grasps
your wrist, you still should be able to move your elbow and shoulder
freely, without destroying your whole body connection. Your fingers
should seek the path of least resistance in which to release the power
of the collision.

A straight line of ki between your one point and that of uke should
be created by your focus. This spiritual connection should be tight,
with no leeway whatsoever. Your physical connection, however, should
be loose, with an ample amount of leeway between yourself and your
partner. The fingers should rise upward into the fire mudra only as
uke's resistance diminishes.

In order for your ki to be strongly extended, it is necessary to release all tension in the joints of the body. When ki is at its maximum extension, the elbows and wrists are slightly bent. If the arms are over-extended, ki extension will return to zero. The fingers show the direction of the ki, yet they follow behind the movement of the wrists.

The wrists, in turn, follow the movement of the waist. In this way the direction of the ki constantly unfolds. "In motion all parts of the body must be light, nimble, and strung together."[2] The fingertips seek the path of least resistance, the direction toward freedom, yet it is the hara that moves first and balances that direction.

Hara alone moves, and the fingers follow like the tail of a comet, lagging behind and dispersing the excess energy generated by the movement. In other words, your fingers should never point directly into the difficulty. The direction of the fingers shows fire ki. It is spiritual as opposed to physical, weak on the outside, with little ability to withstand physical force.

Fire ki gives uke's power a new direction rather than opposing it directly. Water ki should remain passive and follow the lead of fire. Essentially, this means that the amount of tension in the entire body should be equivalent to that required in keeping the hands open. Even in extending the fingers, all the joints of the hand should be free and moveable. It has been taught that it is proper to put a slight amount of tension in one point, yet this leads to sluggish movement and should be avoided.

The legs also should be loose, light, and able to move quickly. Nevertheless, the entire body should be rooted to the earth. An old samurai maxim states, "The body should be heavy, yet the feet should be light." In standing and in movement, your weight should rest above your own feet.

Especially when pivoting, your weight never should be on both feet. If you leave your weight on both feet when they are too far apart, you will be unable to respond to changes in your partner's movement.

The upper body is ruled by Heaven's ki and should float upward naturally. If your body is unified by your ki, your arms will seem to float in the shoulder sockets and the upper body to place no weight on the hips. Practicing this feeling develops A dimension's ki, the ki of Heaven.

Your arms should rest on uke's body by their weight alone. This is the practice of water, or O dimension's ki. Attempting to place your weight on your partner only makes him more stable. Balancing this, the direction of your fingertips branches out horizontally. This is the practice of E dimension's fire ki. In this way the concentration of your natural weight creates a vacuum between uke and you, and he is led down by your one point, or earth ki.

In relaxed movement your weight should remain on the balls of your feet with your heels only lightly touching the mat. The feet move swiftly in *suriashi,* with the large toe in line with the shinbone. Sometimes we see uke stamping his or her feet. This is called *bataashi* and it is not an ideal way of moving. It is better to keep contact with the ground.

Unnecessarily sliding the feet, however, is a mistake. It is not adaptable to the natural terrain of the earth. When you are running fast, your toes should be picked up and the heels allowed to make first contact with the mat.

Holding the body properly with your ki extended, begin forward movement from your hara. The movement of your whole body should be much greater than the movement of your arms. Physical power

■ *Fig. 4.4. Movement of the wrists and hands follows the movement of the hara.*

comes from the earth and is expressed through our hands and arms. "The motion should be rooted in the feet, released through the legs, controlled by the waist, and manifest through the fingers."[3]

The beginner should not attempt to create power when the body is completely stopped. The whole body movement of a master is often undetectable, yet if it is lacking, the ki connection is lost. No one has more ki that anyone else, yet its effectiveness depends on focusing it properly and not obstructing its natural function.

The movement of the hands and arms is created from the rising, sinking, and turning of the body (1). The natural movement of the arms is only extension, retraction, and turning. All other movements involve unnatural force. When sinking the body, the hara sinks downward by releasing the legs. This is followed by the sinking of the wrists and the consequent rising of the fingers (2).

The fingers should always send ki slightly beyond uke's power. The idea is to go around or beyond your partner's power. The ki of your hara, however, should be poured directly into uke's hips. If your hands are free, your mind should be free as well. Even entering directly into uke's resistance, you should be able to find an avenue in which your entire body is able to move freely.

In the words of O-sensei, *The working of the universe is in your legs; the working of the mind is in your hands.* The hips control the lower body. Our power comes from the earth and is distributed by the waist. The hara controls the upper body. The unifying point of these two is your one point. If you receive your partner's power in one point and find a direction toward freedom with your fingers, your movement will be unstoppable.

One point is also the meeting point of tate and yoko. When you learn to breathe, think, and feel from this psychic center, there is no more separation of body and ki. This is not mind over matter, but rather mind and matter as one. It is the method that nature uses exclusively. There should never be any pushing, pulling, lifting, or suppressing, or any manipulation by the arms whatsoever. One point, however, being a function of the mind, is free to break all of these rules.

UKEMI

Finally it is necessary to say something about the art of ukemi. This is the most important tool for learning Aikido. It is only by receiving the feeling of your teacher and your seniors that the direct transmission of Aikido is possible. A great deal of repetition is perhaps a necessary evil inherent in all physical and spiritual disciplines. If this repetition leads to habitual movement rather than a heightened awareness, it can be hard to undo.

The dynamic falls practiced by uke can be a skillful means of escaping from a position of weakness or vulnerability, yet this should not become a habitual response. For the beginner it is excellent physical conditioning, yet in actual self-defense it also can lead to lack of focus.

This problem is especially troublesome due to the feeling of well-being that comes from physical repetition. The student easily becomes addicted to the physical benefits of this kind of conditioning and mistakes it for real understanding. The late Kisaburo Ohsawa at nine dans stated, "If you leave Aikido for three years, it should take you only three days to regain what you have lost."[4]

稽古

■ *Keiko*

For the first three years, a great deal of *renshu,* or repetitive practice, is absolutely essential. This is a kind of misogi, or spiritual purification, which makes you into a vessel for intuitive learning. "It is not possible to learn spontaneity and naturalness. But it is possible to unlearn all of the inhibitive factors which keep you from naturally, effortlessly, being yourself."[5]

If you are still depending on repetition after ten years of practice, you have missed the meaning of Aikido altogether. Within three to ten years the student should go beyond renshu and graduate to *keiko.* The word *keiko* means "to study and embody the wisdom of past ages." This is impossible without a humble and unassuming attitude.

The art of ukemi is the art of receiving, yet this receiving begins with the ability to receive criticism gratefully, and eventually to learn to discover your own mistakes even before they are brought to your attention. Traditionally teachers seldom criticize a student unless they feel that he or she has exceptional potential. A talented student may become a teacher, but if an egocentric attitude is maintained, the art will degenerate.

In the words of the founder: *It seems that modern people think they can master Budo simply by moving the body alone. When I look upon these people who are being trained with this attitude, I feel an inexpressible sorrow along with a great responsibility. A dojo is a place for training in the way, yet present-day dojos are more suited to the term* factories.

The physical practice of receiving begins with the art of falling—learning to receive the mat. You must learn to fall safely and skillfully, yet without opening up a *suki,* or point of vulnerability. The practice of ukemi teaches you to remain mentally centered even when physical balance is lost.

The goal here is to learn to see what is not apparent—to open the mind's eye. It is to develop the ability to intuit your opponent's movement before it has been made. A moment of reflection will reveal that this ability is, in fact, essential to the art of self-defense. Harmony is the most impenetrable of all defenses. If you read your partner's intention, you will be able to move together with attack.

Developing this kind of sensitivity also means being able to escape from danger before it occurs. For this reason the ukemi practice of Aikido may appear as allowing defeat. Rather, it is escaping from what has not yet happened. On the other hand, if it is your partner who opens up a suki, the harmonious thing to do is to fill that opening with atemi, a strike, or *kaeshi waza,* a reversal of the technique.

Aikido is a noncompetitive martial art. There are no rules such as those in karate or judo competitions. It is necessary, therefore, to take seriously all of the possibilities open to your partner and to be responsible for defending against them. If this attitude is lost, the spiritual as well as the martial value of Aikido training ceases to exist. There is no possibility of an effective defense without the possibility of offense.

Aikido has sometimes been described as *sente no nai budo,* or the martial way that doesn't initiate offense. This doesn't mean, however, that you should wait for the attack and attempt to blend with it. Such an attitude leads to action-reaction and a physical collision of force. "If others move slightly, I move first."[6]

Practically speaking, it would be impossible to lead or blend with your partner's ki without the potential of atemi. Entering directly with atemi, change your partner's intention. At this moment his offense becomes defense. It is his defensive movement with which you should blend.

If you attempt to blend with your partner's attack, you will be assisting his attempt to strike you. If, on the other hand, you oppose it directly, the result likely will be the same. The way of Aikido is to react to your opponent's intention before it takes physical form. The founder stated, *The one who even considers attacking me has already lost; he is disrupting the order of the universe.*

The goal in Aikido is to reach the level where an actual strike is unnecessary; it is to be able to lead your partner's mind by your own awareness of that possibility. According to the founder, however, in an actual confrontation, 70 percent is atemi, 30 percent is technique. In daily practice, therefore, you should study the various atemi relating to each technique.

Through the art of ukemi the student eventually comes to understand the futility of both competition and rigidity. It is necessary to eliminate tightness from both body and mind. As long as you carry a feeling of competition, you will be caught up in action-reaction. This makes productive practice impossible. Good ukemi is neither obstinacy nor compliance, but rather listening and blending.

When you are forced down you should always receive nage's power in your hara and then bend from the waist. Always bend to the side, never directly backward or forward. It is somewhat like a tightrope walker leaning from side to side as he moves forward. In this way you will learn to use the power of hara rather than the small power of your arms. When forced downward, sink your entire body rather than resisting with your shoulders or legs. Resistance causes the movement to stagnate and allows your partner to strike you.

The early students of the founder were already masters of other martial arts, yet the founder did not allow any physical resistance before three years of training, or the level of sandan. For those who begin without martial expertise, this becomes ten years of training. The beginner is not aware of the possibilities open to his partner, and his resistance is therefore meaningless.

On the other hand, uke is responsible for delivering a meaningful attack. If the attack is unrealistic or lacking in vitality, your partner will not be able to practice proper kokyu and timing. The attack should be carried out instantaneously, with a momentary tension and immediate release of that tension at the moment of contact. "Store up internal strength like drawing a bow (fire). Release it like releasing an arrow (water)."[7]

The release of tension not only prepares you for receiving and blending with nage's power; it also frees you up for a second attack. If you maintain tension after your attack, you will be unable to adapt to your partner's response.

When grasping your partner's wrist, avoid pressing your palm firmly against his body. This stops the extension of your own ki. Your grasp should always emphasize either the fire or the water side of your hand, with your palm only lightly touching. Pushing inward, use the water mudra. Pulling back, use the little finger and fire mudra.

When your partner strikes with speed and power, there is a tendency to freeze and react from your shoulders. This fear of being hit should be replaced by a feeling of transparency. Do not stand your ground and block, but rather move out of the way of the attack and lead your partner's ki. Japanese castles often had a moat surrounding them so that the enemy could not attack. Our mind itself can become the water separating us from attack. O-sensei taught, *Use the tip of your enemy's spear as your shield.*

The art of ukemi is the art of life. As human beings we should be the most sensitive receivers of all. Learning to receive and carry the ki of your partner is essential for ki-musubi, and therefore for all Aikido techniques. This carrying of ki is the sacred syllable of Aum or Om. It is the vibration of the universe manifesting itself.

Master Ueshiba would begin his *kagura mai,* or dance of the gods, by chanting *Omoomoomu* several times. He explained that with the sound of O and U he was expressing the beginning of natural movement. The ki of O, merging with the rhythm of M, also creates the kototama of Mo. Mo has the function of bringing kototama closer to each other and holding them together. In Aikido terms, this is the activity of ki-musubi.

THE SPIRIT OF IKKYO

Ikkyo, Irimi nage, and Shiho nage are the three pillars of Aikido. Ikkyo—literally, "the first teaching"—is the simplest, most bare-bones example of suberu, the spiral principle of Aikido. The entire movement of Ikkyo unfolds as Su-A-I-E-To-Su. Ikkyo is the de-ai, the meeting point of two forces.

The symbol of Su (shown in the first chapter) shows your partner's center and the periphery of the technique. With your hara focused directly into uke's center, hi no te and mizu no te lead uke's ki into a void. It is like the Biblical expression, "A wheel in the middle of a wheel." In other words, the spiral form created by tate and yoko leads uke off balance so that he can be brought down with a few ounces of pressure.

Coming forth with the ki of nonresistence manifests the kototama of Su. Rising up from one point and expanding is Ya. A is water ki within the empty sky of U dimension. I is the center of that ki, which gives it motion. E dimension's ki branches out horizontally, while O dimension's ki rides on uke's center with the natural weight of the body alone.

Maintaining the balance of the eight powers, we pass through the center of the technique with effortless grace. This is the kototama of To-Su.

■ *A symbolic representation of Ikkyo*

■ Ikkyo

In spiritual terms, the kototama of To-Su is the ki of effortlessly crossing over to the other shore. It is *satori,* or the clarity of enlightenment.

Manifesting the futonorito order of the vowels in this way maintains the perfect balance of one spirit, four souls, three origins, and eight powers as you move effortlessly through the technique. In the words of Yamaguchi Seigo sensei, "There is only tate, yoko, naname, and tsuki. There is nothing outside of vertical, horizontal, diagonal, and thrusting through the center." The dynamic balance of tate and yoko creates naname, the diagonal form of your arm movement. Passing through the center provides the continual source of ki to your arms.

Shomen Uchi Ikkyo (Ryutai)

Entering: The De-Ai

As explained in chapter 3 on kokyu, there are three stages to each technique: receiving, carrying, and releasing the ki. Entering is the most important part of any Aikido technique. In Aikido, you enter for the purpose of receiving your partner's power in your one point. As you enter, reach your arms out and draw his ki into your hara (1).

You should align your hips with those of your partner as he attacks and then, sinking downward, receive his ki on the vertical plane (tate). When you receive properly you internalize uke's power and give it a new direction (2). As you receive uke's power, guide it upward and out of his body.

Your body moves directly into uke, yet there must be no pushing whatsoever. A true master is always the receiver. In this way you establish unity and unbalance your partner immediately. The sinking of your body and the rising of your arms should be simultaneous (3, 4). This is the correct way to manifest the powers of Hi and Ni, Heaven and Earth.

■ *Fig. 4.5. De-ai: entering*

■ *Fig. 4.6. Establish whole body unity and
unbalance your partner immediately.*

■ *Fig. 4.7. Sinking and rising ki—hips and arms moving in opposition*

■ *Fig. 4.8. Turn toward uke's strike.*

■ *Fig. 4.9. Control uke by controlling the space around him.*

When your partner strikes, simply turn your body in the direction of his arm. In this way you will draw his power out of his arm even as you advance toward his omote, which is his weakest point of balance (1, 2). Rather than trying to control your partner's body or arm by direct manipulation, control his movement by controlling the space around him (3).

■ *Fig. 4.10. Kiri oroshi attack met with scissors*

A Variation of Receiving

If uke attacks with *kiri oroshi,* or a strong strike from above, there is a tendency to receive his descending arm with your palms. Rather, adjust your *ma-ai,* or distance, and raise your arm with the form of Kokyu undo. Your rising hand should create a scissors effect with his descending arm. When this is performed properly, you will slide on top of uke's strike without any solid contact whatsoever.

Tai-sabaki: Judgment in Motion

In the teachings of the founder we find, *The first movement of Aikido technique is tsuki.* First of all, this indicates the direct lines of I dimension's ki reaching straight out from our hara in all directions. However, it also refers to actually thrusting forward with our body.

Having received uke's ki and taken it into our hara, our body again rises up to ride on uke's center. Our arms lead uke's ki out of his body, yet our hips continue to face directly into uke's center. Balancing the movement of the hips, the hand of fire (E) thrusts forward with a spiral motion toward uke's face. Never push uke's arm to the side; this allows him to escape and strike you. Rather, let the turning of your arm lead him out.

Thrusting and turning, the hand of fire naturally rises upward and then branches out and down toward uke's hara. Once again from the *Kototama Hissho: The ki of fire is originally in the heavenly realm, yet branching outward it sinks down to the earth.*

Balancing the branching (yoko) movement of the hand of fire, the hand of water turns over to ride on top of uke's arm and therefore rise up vertically (tate). *The ki of water is originally of the earth, yet rising upward it cycles in the heavens.*

It should be noted here that although the thrusting motion of the arms is created mainly from the forward movement of the body, there should be no pushing whatsoever. Pushing is the most common mistake in trying to perform Ikkyo and it is also the most difficult problem to eliminate.

The realm of tai-sabaki is where the form of the technique is mainly created; therefore, the motion of the arms should be explained in more detail at this time. Asked about the essence of swordsmanship, O-sensei replied, *Of course, it is cutting and thrusting!* Aside from the face value of this statement, there is a deeper meaning here.

Thrusting (*tsuki*) and cutting (*kiru*) in Aikido are not two separate motions, but rather two sides of one principle. Thrusting is tate, and cutting is yoko. As you pass through the movement of Ikkyo, the thrusting motion of your arms continually must clear the way for them to fall.

The hand of fire always leads the movement from the beginning to the end of the technique. It never exerts physical force but rather follows the path of least resistance. The hand of water follows behind as if being drawn into a vacuum. It is important to note here that water ki doesn't follow behind fire ki in position only. It begins its motion slightly after fire ki has already initiated movement. It is like swinging your arms from side to side; the first hand almost finishes the movement before the other begins.

Your two hands are like generals going out into battle as decoys to deter the attack away from hara, the lord. In the end, it is one point alone that brings uke down. This is possible because all the difficulty has already been removed; one point has no power of its own.

■ *Fig. 4.11. The hand of fire directs ki away from uke's center, while the hand of water directs ki inward.*

Both hands should touch uke's arm as lightly as possible, allowing the emphasis to fall on the invisible connection of hara-to-hara. The movement of your two hands together thrusts forward and opens the door for your hara to enter directly. As fire and water ki open the door, earth ki passes through the center and unifies them.

Hi no te (yoko) takes uke's elbow outside and away from his own center, while mizu no te (tate) redirects his ki inward and toward his center. Mizu no te, associated with the earth, acts as a medium for the ki of your hara to reach uke's center. These two blending together create a spiral movement, or triangle form, entering into uke's hara. The combined function of both hands, however, is to take uke's ki out of his body. This is in contrast to the hara, which sends ki directly into uke's hara, causing his ki to rise.

If hi no te continues to lead properly, there will be no stopping and mizu no te will not receive uke's weight and be forced into pushing. The ki of water manifests movement as power, yet water never pushes down on the earth. Following the path of least resistance, it seeks the lowest resting place. When power remains still and in reserve, it manifests higher judgment and wisdom.

■ *Fig. 4.12. Handblade on the neck*

■ *Fig. 4.13. Kesa giri*

The movement of Aikido is fundamentally the same as that of the sword. Turning your body as you thrust through the center of uke's movement, the ki extension of your handblade will descend across the line of uke's neck. This mimics the *kesa giri* cut. Just as with the sword, your arms reach out, yet they draw uke's ki inward as you move through the technique.

Always try to control the joint just above the place of physical contact. As your fire hand controls uke's elbow through vertical extension, your water hand should control his shoulder through horizontal turning. This is done not by pushing directly into it but rather by turning it inside and toward his hara. There should be no direct manipulation of uke's arm.

The power of Aikido technique appears to be created by the arms, yet it is actually generated by the legs, hips, and hara. The proper use of your legs, hips, and hara eliminates the problem of overextending the arms. The power generated by the legs and hips should be invisible to the

■ *Fig. 4.14. Hanmi handachi ikkyo*

naked eye, yet difficult to stop. Aikido, therefore, appears to be either fake or magic. With training we come to understand that it is neither.

Nage and Osae

It is almost unavoidable that the beginning student will set a goal of being able to throw his or her partner successfully. The problem is that even more advanced students seem to maintain this attitude, as if it were some criterion of actual ability. In reality, if your focus is on throwing, your Aikido in not applicable to actual self-defense.

Attempting to throw your partner, you are at your most vulnerable. Throwing is an idea left over from the early roots of Aikido, yet Aikido doesn't really lend itself to throwing in the manner of judo or even jujutsu. The Koshi nage of judo are excellent training for developing the hips and legs, yet beyond that they are not usually considered to be essential techniques for studying Aikido.

Rather than *nage,* or throwing, Aikido concentrates on *osae,* bringing your partner's defenses down and exposing his vulnerability. Even

■ *Fig. 4.15. To-Su and inori: passing through the technique leads uke's ki horizontally out of his arm.*

putting too much emphasis on successfully bringing uke down misses the point. The emphasis in Aikido technique should be on passing through the movement unhindered.

Following the pattern of earth, fire, water, and again earth, your arms follow uke's descent naturally without pushing or pulling. When this is accomplished, uke will fall exactly where he stands.

In the words of O-sensei, we find the proper attitude for finishing Aikido technique: *Bring your partner down in the sign of the square.*

Study the way of moving uke's body without disrupting his arms whatsoever. When you find direct hara-to-hara contact, uke's entire body will sink. When he attempts to raise his arms to defend his face, his whole body will be controlled. When he is brought down in this way, ideally you should pass through the technique peacefully. The key word is *o-ryoki,* which means "just enough." It is economy of movement that creates both effectiveness and beauty.

■ *Fig. 4.16. Adjusting your one point to maintain control*

To-Su (passing through) and *inori* (riding on your partner's ki) are the main ingredients of Aikido technique. Having entered properly, do not reverse the direction of your hips, but move straight forward with your new direction. The key point here is that the hand of water should always be passive.

Continually passing through the movement keeps uke off balance and unable to find stable ground. If you push down you will reach the bottom of the technique. This gives uke back his legs and allows him to regain his balance. By leading uke's ki horizontally out of his arm, you can maintain control (1, 2). As uke struggles to get up, continue to maintain control by adjusting the focus of your one point (3, 4).

■ *Fig. 4.17. Suwari waza ikkyo: bring the legs together as you rise up.*

Suwari Waza Ikkyo

Suwari waza, a technique done on your knees, is especially important as it allows the student to study upper body movement without falling into the common mistake of evasiveness. It is also an extremely valuable method for developing hips and legs, the source of Aikido power. Moving from the seated posture of seiza, bring the legs together as you rise up on your knees, toes bent under as if you were about to stand (1).

There are three steps in the basic form of omote. The first step is to establish the proper ma-ai, or distance. It begins with *ai-hanmi.* When your partner strikes with *shomen uchi,* advance to his omote with ai-hanmi. The other side of your body should actually retreat in order to receive uke's power. Your emphasis should be on striking atemi to uke's ribs, rather than on moving his striking arm (2).

It is important to receive uke's power correctly. Turn your hips in the direction of his attacking arm and let the hand of fire thrust forward until your arm rests on top of uke's strike (3). By sliding on top of uke's descending arm, you avoid collision.

The second step moves directly into uke's center and takes him off balance. As the hand of water rises upward, you should rotate it to the top of his arm rather than receiving his weight with your palm. This helps avoid the common mistake of pushing.

■ *Fig. 4.18. The basic form of omote*

Your third step leads uke out of his hara with the hand of fire, as the hand of water allows your natural weight to ride on his center and bring him down (4). There should be no grasping of uke's wrist until the end of the technique. Maintain the fire mudra as you grasp. It is only when uke shows the palm side of his hand that the Yonkyo grasp is applied.

■ Fig. 4.19. Maintain fire mudra as you grasp (1 shows the incorrect form and 2 the correct form).

■ Fig. 4.20. A passive water hand successfully blocks uke's kick.

The most common mistake in Ikkyo is pushing with the hand of water. This exposes you to a variety of counterattacks, especially a roundhouse kick (1). If your water hand remains the passive receiver of uke's ki (2), you can easily let it slide down and stop uke's kick (3, 4, 5, 6).

Suwari Waza Ikkyo Ura

Suwari waza ikkyo ura shows two very important points about technique in general. First of all, it clearly shows how all Aikido techniques begin with the omote form. *Omote* means "positive" or yang ki or direct confrontation. *Ura,* on the other hand, is yin or evasiveness. Beginning a technique with an evasive attitude is weak and usually will fail. Attempting to enter directly behind your partner is never successful in a real situation.

Omote refers to basic technique, and ura is a more advanced application. In a sense we can say that ura is the continuation of omote. In omote techniques you should enter directly into the technique and control from the inside. Ura techniques begin by entering with omote and then using tenkan to escape to the outside of uke's attack and control from that position.

Entering, the first stage of technique, should always begin with omote. In order to avoid the potential atemi to his face, uke is forced to raise his elbow toward the outside of his body. His elbow becomes a "floating point" within the triangle of wrist, elbow, and hara (1).

■ *Fig. 4.21. The elbow becomes a floating point.*

■ *Fig. 4.22. Using the entrance point as a pivot point for turning*

■ *Fig. 4.23. When leading
with hi no te, uke can
be moved without any
pulling.*

Entering into Ikkyo omote, the manner of lining up your hips with your partner is unchanged from the form described in the section on Kokyu ho. The ki of your right hip should enter into the right hip of your partner (2). In changing to the ura form, however, use that entrance point also as a pivot point for your tenkan movement.

The second point, which is well illustrated in Ikkyo ura, is the importance of the fire hand in leading the movement. Hi no te should continually lead uke's movement, even if physical contact is lost (3). If

■ *Fig. 4.24. Mizu no te leads uke's ki out of his body. Hi no te rides on top of his attack.*

■ *Fig. 4.25. Uke is led off balance by the hand of fire.*

you revert to trying to move uke with your water hand or attempt to physically pull with hi no te, you will fail.

By maintaining the arc created by uke's bending arm and allowing your natural weight to be transferred to uke through the water hand, hara-to-hara contact with uke can be established and uke can be moved without any pulling whatsoever (4). This relationship of omote to ura should be researched in all Aikido techniques.

Katate Tori Ikkyo

Katate tori ikkyo presents a very useful set of difficulties, each with lessons to teach. Uke's grasp pushes directly down on your arm, making it impossible to oppose his force directly. Your grasped hand is mizu no te, yet due to the nature of the attack, it takes the role of fire and leads uke's ki out of his body.

Hi no te is free and threatens atemi, yet at the beginning of this technique it takes the role of water and rides on top of uke's attack. Here we have a classic example of fire within water, and water within fire.

At the moment of contact, your weight should shift to your forward foot, thereby putting power into the hand of water. Receiving uke's ki, bring it up the back of your spine, thereby causing his ki to rise. He is then led off balance by the hand of fire.

■ *Fig. 4.26. The water mudra sends uke's ki upward.*

Because mizu no te is confronted with uke's power, there is a tendency to respond directly and miss the importance of hi no te. Hi no te must lead the movement by taking uke's arm horizontally outward, thereby allowing mizu no te to send ki vertically upward to ride on top of uke's arm. Sinking into the movement, send uke's ki upward with the water mudra.

■ *Fig. 4.27. Extend the hand of water to spiral around uke's thumb. Notice the direction of the fingers away from uke's power.*

As you extend the hand of water, let it spiral inward around uke's thumb until it rides on top of his arm. Remember that the feeling of extension (tate) must always exceed the feeling of turning (yoko). Notice the direction of the fingers away from uke's power. Each of your arms has its own function, yet the two should move as one. The small movement of the hand of fire makes the extension of the hand of water successful.

As in all Aikido techniques, the formula is the same. The complementary function of your two hands gives them freedom to move as if in a void. Their combined function opens the door for hara to pass through the technique. The real power of the movement comes completely from your legs and is distributed by your waist.

Shugyo: The Spiritual Training of Technique

■ *Fig. 4.28. Men tsuki ikkyo omote: Ikkyo in response to a face punch*

Men Tsuki Ikkyo Omote

Ikkyo as a response to a face punch (*men tsuki*) shows the role of *gedan* as a defensive posture. If you attempt to receive the punch with your hands raised, you will be unable to lead your partner's ki. Keeping your arms down as if holding a sword in gedan, you will easily rise up to meet the attack. This particular Ikkyo also makes it very clear that any pushing whatsoever is counterproductive. You must learn to mold your partner's form as you receive it.

■ *Fig. 4.29. Men tsuki ikkyo ura in the kotai form*

Men Tsuki Ikkyo Ura

In order to grasp the ura form, you should first see it as *kotai,* or basic form. When your partner strikes your solar plexus, use the fire mudra to bring his arm down (1, 2) and then strike his face with your blocking arm (3). If he is able to block your strike, use his block to perform Ikkyo. The movement is finished with the standard Ikkyo nage (4, 5).

■ *Fig. 4.30. Men tsuki ikkyo ura in the abbreviated ryutai form*

Once this is understood you can abbreviate, as in the ryutai form. The movements of the block are covered by your focus alone, and you enter directly into the striking position. This will be very difficult if you have not mastered the basic form first. If you have any fear of being hit, you probably will be. The finish is the same as in the kotai form above.

Gyakute

Gyakute literally means "to turn the wrist against its natural direction of movement." It is a term taken from jujutsu and is not really applicable to Aikido. Complying with Aikido principle, twisting the joint is a mistake. Twisting the joint causes pain, yet it doesn't necessarily control uke's body or stop him from launching a counterattack. Turning the joint is a horizontal movement (yoko) and must therefore follow behind the extension (tate) of the joint. In this way the tendons between the joints are extended and controlled with a minimum of pressure.

Although Chinese kung fu contains hundreds of gyakute (*chin na*) movements, the founder of Aikido emphasized only three variations of Ikkyo. Moving from one to the next as a progression, they take on philosophical meaning. Ikkyo is a perfect sphere, or *tama,* representing pure polarity, the original undifferentiated spirit. Nikyo is created by drawing ki to the inside of that sphere, creating the spiral of materialization.

As contraction reaches its extreme, the spiral begins to expand again in the Sankyo technique. Eventually that expansion reaches its extreme and turns back in upon itself. This is *motogaeri,* returning to the origin, the teaching of Yonkyo.

Although these are among the most basic of Aikido techniques, they are mastered to the point of being effective only after many years of training. As a result, they are often learned and then disregarded as simplistic or ineffective. The reality, however, is that these are the first alternatives in a real self-defense situation. They are an intermediate stage between strikes and can eliminate the need for grappling.

Kata Tori Nikyo

In Aikido gyakute techniques, the way of grasping correctly is essential. You should grasp below the wrist, rather than on the wrist itself. Unless there is play in uke's wrist, his resistance will succeed. In order to control any joint, therefore, your contact should be below that joint.

If your contact is above uke's wrist, you must control his elbow. If it is above his elbow, you will have to control his shoulder. If your contact is with the trunk of his body, as in Irimi nage, you must control his hara directly. In Nikyo and Sankyo you should grasp in such as way as to also control uke's thumb. When you control his earth ki directly, he will not be able to resist.

■ *Fig. 4.31. Motogaeri: returning to the source (Artwork by Cynthia Zoppa)*

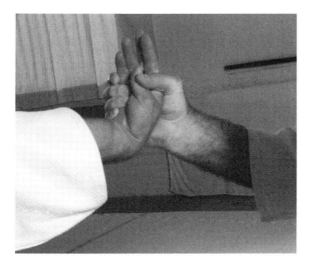

■ *Fig. 4.32. Kata tori nikyo: control uke's thumb by grasping below the wrist, rather than on the wrist.*

■ *Fig. 4.33. Controlling uke's wrist with the Kata tori nikyo technique*

In the Kata tori nikyo ura technique, uke's strongest defense is to extend his arm and push directly into you. In this way his wrist is tight and protected from pain or damage. If you use your hip movement to draw the tightness out of uke's wrist vertically (tate), your opposite hand will be able turn his wrist horizontally (yoko) (1). When we control uke's wrist and hand, we control his or her mind.

This also gives you a potential atemi (2). Even as you draw the ki out of his arm, your hara sends ki directly into his hara.

Even in a contracting technique such as Nikyo, you should hold your partner's body almost the way you would hold a small child. Your feeling should encompass, rather than kill, uke's ki. Contrary to what would seem obvious, if you hold tightly, your partner will escape more easily.

■ *Fig. 4.34. Use the thumb as a pivot point to bring uke down.*

Shomen Uchi Nikyo: Ura Movement

When uke is brought down with Ikkyo, he will attempt to rise up and attack again. Your water hand keeps him from rising while your fire hand, using the thumb as a pivot point, grasps in the Nikyo position (3). Pushing down on uke's arm is a mistake. The less pressure placed on his arm, the better. If your emphasis remains on adjusting uke's balance with a horizontal movement (yoko) from above (tate), he will be controlled with a small amount of pressure from your natural weight (4). Using the thumb as a pivot point, grasp in the Nikyo position and bring uke down.

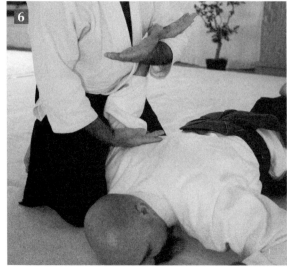

■ *Fig. 4.35. Complete the pin by securing uke's arm. Note that the variation shown in photo 6 is not recommended.*

In completing the pin, there are several steps. As you bring uke's arm up to your body, the hand of water should bend his elbow. It is important that uke is completely held down by the hand of water alone, while the hand of fire is positioned (5).

Sometimes students will attempt to tuck uke's palm into their elbow joint. Frankly, the difficulty of getting this grasp is hardly worth the effort. Attempting it may cause you to lose control altogether (6).

Rather, simply place your hand across uke's arm or, if more power is necessary, grasp your own garment and lean into uke's arm in the direction of his head (7). Uke's arm should take the form of an arc. If it is bent too much or left too straight, he will escape easily.

■ *Fig. 4.36. Grasping uke's fingers, a step intermediate to Sankyo*

■ *Fig. 4.37. The finger grip can be used to bring uke down immediately.*

Shomen Uchi Sankyo Omote

The basic method of grasping Sankyo also begins from the Ikkyo position. If uke is trying to escape, he will present you with the back of his hand. This leads naturally to the Nikyo grasp seen above. If he is trying to push against you, he will more likely show you his palm. In this case you can grasp his fingers, an intermediary step to Sankyo.

This kind of grasp is not for the purpose of twisting the fingers, but rather to extend the tendons of the arm. It also can be used to bring uke down immediately, if necessary.

■ *Fig. 4.38. Sankyo omote*

Stepping to uke's omote and extending your arm, push uke's elbow to his diagonal in order to unbalance him (1). Grasp Sankyo with your opposite hand and turn his palm away from you (2, 3). Do not attempt to turn his wrist (yoko) without extending (tate). It is the act of extending the arm that makes it possible to turn his palm away from you.

As you continue to move to uke's omote, the turning of your hips becomes the power for bringing him down, yet the extension of his arm continues to lead the movement (4, 5).

The proper Sankyo grasp, once again, should be slightly below the wrist. As in Nikyo, the important thing is to control the thumb. In Sankyo this is done with the middle joint of your thumb in a position to apply pressure to the point behind uke's thumb.

■ *Fig. 4.39. The turning of nage's hips brings uke down.*

■ *Fig. 4.40. Apply pressure to the point behind uke's thumb with the middle joint of your thumb.*

If you hold too high or into uke's wrist, it is easy for him to drop his elbow and do Kokyu nage. You should extend all uke's joints by raising his ki up with your hara. When you are holding properly and with relaxed arms, a slight movement of your hips will transfer sufficient power to accomplish the technique.

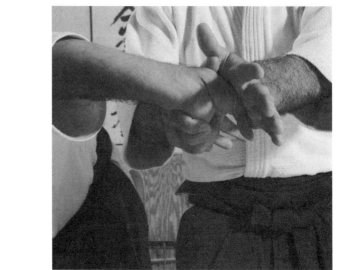

■ *Fig. 4.41. Sankyo grip for nage whose hands are smaller than uke's.*

There is sometimes a problem when nage has comparatively small hands and is practicing with a larger partner. In this case, line up your opposite hand perpendicular to your partner's hand and roll your thumb toward uke's palm. Even the largest opponent will be unable to resist.

Yonkyo

One of the most common explanations of Aikido is "using your partner's power against him." This has become a cliché, yet it is still true. The question then becomes, "How is it actually done?" In order to use another person's energy against him, it is necessary, first of all, to unite with that energy and actually incorporate it into your own body until there is no separation.

The main point is that you must cause uke to push into your hand and receive his power in your hara and legs. As you allow his pushing to enter directly into your hara, he will be moved.

If you push into your partner's power, he will resist you easily. The pressure put on uke's arm can be painful, yet it will not stop a determined adversary. The first two steps are the same as in the Sankyo technique above, except that uke's entire hand is grasped slightly below the wrist. This makes it comfortable to apply the water mudra just above his wrist.

▪ Fig. 4.42. Yonkyo: move uke by allowing his pushing on your hand to enter directly into your hara.

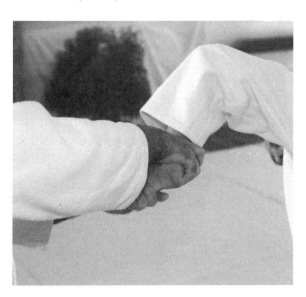

▪ Fig. 4.43. Grasp uke's entire hand slightly below the wrist and apply the water mudra just above the wrist.

■ *Fig. 4.44. One-handed Yonkyo: when grasped from two sides, nage can use Yonkyo to turn his adversaries against each other.*

This effectiveness of this approach can be demonstrated by practicing a one-handed Yonkyo with each of your arms being grasped. If you are receiving properly, you will be able to control both sides and use their movements against each other.

入り身投げ

THE SPIRIT OF IRIMI NAGE

As the spirit of Ikkyo strives to emanate the kototama of Su, Irimi nage characterizes the kototama of Su-A, entering and opening. As the sister technique to Ikkyo, however, it also embodies the entire kototama progression of AIEOU. Entering directly with the ki of Su, your body opens (A) as you pivot to avoid uke's strike.

As always, the tightly wound ki of I, the activity of one point, remains hidden. The hand of fire (E) leads uke's ki outward, giving it new direction, while the hand of water (O) rests at the top of his spine, creating ki-musubi. This is, once again, the futonorito order of the vowel dimensions.

As Ikkyo is associated with the triangle and the direct entering of omote, the usual practice of Irimi nage is associated with the circle and the turning movement of ura techniques. This easily leads to a mistaken impression about the spirit of Irimi nage. The visible form of Irimi nage strives to manifest the circle of Su-A-I, the form of perfect harmony. The invisible spirit behind this form, however, is extremely severe.

Aikido is originally a battlefield martial art; therefore it is effectiveness, rather than beauty, that is essential. Beauty has value only when it is the result of correct movement and principle. In the words of R. Buckminster Fuller, "When I'm working on a problem, I never think about beauty. I think only how to solve the problem. But when I have finished, if the solution is not beautiful, I know it is wrong."[8]

In other words, the beautiful and flowing form of Irimi nage is created from a very practical and direct entering into your partner's attack. The spirit of Irimi nage is fundamentally linear; it is not a technique of escape or unnecessarily opening the body. In the words of Yamaguchi Seigo sensei, *The spirit of Irimi is* ai-uchi, *or choosing death in order to live.*

In Japanese sword it is expressed as *Sei shi kami ichi mai,* "The difference between life and death is the thickness of a sheet of paper." It is with this attitude that Irimi nage should be approached. Entering with a strong sense of omote, lead uke's attack out and then, at the last minute, avoid it by tenkan. *If your opponent strikes with fire, counter with water, becoming completely fluid and free flowing.*

Irimi nage is almost always practiced as an ura form. For this reason it is essential to enter with a strong sense of omote before turning to avoid uke's strike. In this sense Irimi nage is very similar to Ikkyo ura. Even when there isn't time to enter into the omote position, the mind of entering must be present. Omote changing into ura as you enter takes the form of the letter *S*, the symbol of nonresistance or unobstructed movement.

In the Irimi nage technique, this form is created when both people, moving in opposite directions, merge together and cycle around each other. In this way we can see that the letter *S* inside a circle creates the symbol of yin and yang, the origin of movement. Your forward movement passing through the center of this symbol creates the kototama form of To-Su.

The founder referred to this mutual integration as the dance of the deities Izanagi no kami and Izanami no kami. In their courting ritual, these deities circle in opposite directions around a vertical pillar until they meet and unite. As described in chapter 2, this is the process of *karami,* winding around each other and unifying the vertical ki of I and Wi, the life will and power.

■ *Fig. 4.45. The letter S inside a circle creates the symbol of yin and yang.*

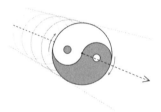

■ *Fig. 4.46. The kototama form of To-Su*

■ *Fig. 1.47. Izanagi no kami and Izanami no kami circle in opposite directions around a vertical pillar until they meet and are united.*

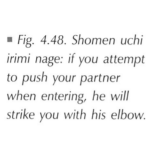

■ *Fig. 4.48. Shomen uchi irimi nage: if you attempt to push your partner when entering, he will strike you with his elbow.*

Shomen Uchi Irimi Nage (Ryutai)

Entering

In all Aikido techniques, the *ryutai,* or flowing form, is the most important daily practice. As with Ikkyo, the shomen uchi attack is also the most important way of practicing Irimi nage. When performed with speed and accuracy, this attack forces nage to learn the proper feeling and form for entering. If you attempt to push your partner's attack aside, he will strike you with his elbow.

When contact is made, simply roll your wrist against his arm and he will be unable to free himself for a strike. Your focus should be on moving uke's feet, rather than his arm. Your tenkan (pivot) should be completed before you place your weight on the opposite foot. In this way you are ready for the next movement immediately.

■ *Fig. 4.49. Upon contact, simply roll your wrist against his arm.*

■ *Fig. 4.50. Complete your tenkan before shifting weight to the opposite foot.*

■ *Fig. 4.51. The triangle method, sankaku ho, done with swords*

Ideally, however, you should avoid contact altogether. Sankaku ho, the triangle method, is shown here with the sword. Entering directly with an upward cutting, or *kiriage,* movement shows the essence of omote feeling. It is a direct and offensive confrontation (1, 2, 3). Lacking the constant potential of offense, Irimi nage, in a real situation with a knife or sword, would be nothing short of suicide.

As his sword descends, step to his forward diagonal and cut *kiri orosu,* or diagonally downward (4, 5). If he enters more deeply, your pivot is greater and the sword is placed at the back of his neck. Connecting your beginning and ending position to uke's original position reveals the triangle form.

■ *Fig. 4.52. Sankaku ho, done barehanded*

In barehanded technique the sword becomes the mind, instantly cutting upward and drawing uke inward when he attacks (1). Cutting upward and then down, like the opening and closing of an umbrella, you appear to enter behind uke, yet the reality is that he passes in front of you. When his strike misses you, you will already be standing behind him (2).

If there is any feeling of trying to escape from uke's attack, there will be no offense and you will never reach the second movement. If you attempt to enter behind uke by moving to his forward diagonal, you will not escape. It is much like a hunter training his sights on a flying duck. It is an easy and predictable target.

Without a strong feeling of omote, ura cannot succeed. It is a mistake to wait for your partner to attack and then attempt to blend with his movement. This would be to assist in your own destruction. Aikido is not such a simple-minded practice as that. When your partner's mind is set on attacking, enter with atemi. In this way you create your partner's timing and then blend with his response. Without this yang or positive attitude, blending with a malicious attack is impossible.

The principle of irimi-tenkan dictates that all Aikido techniques are fundamentally linear (tate), with turning or circular movement (yoko) existing only to assist forward movement. In Irimi nage, pivoting should be accomplished in a moment, yet your feeling should continue to enter. A slight feeling of tension, or torque from turning, should be maintained in the hips at all times.

Tai-sabaki

An old Zen story tells of two monks discussing whether it is the wind that moves the trees or the trees that move the wind. The moral of the story is that there is no separation, but nevertheless there is a difference. In our present society, people act as if the tree is moving the wind. They see only that which is physical and apparent as the cause of movement and power.

Common sense, however, would dictate that the wind is the larger force and moves the trees. Until we learn to see the world of ki and spirit as the source of our power, the reality of Aikido will not reveal itself. In proper Aikido movement it is that which appears to be stationary that is, in fact, really moving.

Understanding this, we should eliminate all the pushing and pulling commonly seen in Irimi nage and replace it with body movement. As you move your body closer and farther away from uke, your connection with his hara remains undisturbed.

Tai-sabaki is the transition from forward movement to turning. In other words, it is the juncture of the irimi-tenkan principle. Discussing the proper use of tenkan, therefore, is a good place to shift your focus from entering to that of tai-sabaki.

Even before contact we are unified by ki and consciousness. The process of creation continually alternates between unity and separation. Following this principle of nature, our physical coming together should be followed immediately by separation. This manifests the kototama of Ha-A-Wa-Ya.

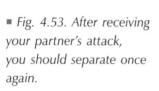
■ *Fig. 4.53. After receiving your partner's attack, you should separate once again.*

This pattern is essential in Aikido techniques. First there is unity before separation, the ki of Su-U. In receiving your partner's attack, unity should be established. Following that, you should once again create space by moving away from uke. Expanding your body is different from pushing. Make no effort to move uke with your arms. Attempting to pull uke down is the most common mistake made in doing Irimi nage. Rather, cause his ki to rise as your ki thrusts straight down through his center.

Gathering energy into your body is also different from pulling. Once you have created space between uke and yourself, manifest the kototama of Ya by rising up into the common space that unites you. As hands and hips come together once again, there is no change in the intensity of contact with uke. The more lightly you touch uke's body, the greater will be the potential influence of your hara-to-hara contact. It is this standing in the center and opening that brings uke down without any pushing or pulling.

When used for adding power to forward movement, the turning of your hips should be so gradual as to be imperceptible. When used to avoid a strike, it should be sharp and sudden. If you emphasize vertical feeling, your weight will remain above your feet and you will be able to

■ Fig. 4.54. Kototama of Ya: standing in the center and opening brings uke down.

move your legs freely. If you attempt to pull your partner down, your legs will become tight and uke will turn easily and strike you.

Above controls below, and when you learn to see your partner from above, he can be controlled with a minimum of effort. "A stone weighing several thousand pounds is extremely heavy. But although it is heavy from below, it is easy to manipulate the stone from above."[9] In Aikido we attempt not to become strong, but rather to eliminate the need for power.

Osae/Nage

The separation of hands and hips should occur vertically as well as horizontally. Sinking your body, don't attempt to pull uke down. Rather let mizu no te rest at the top of uke's spine. Send his ki upward (tate) even as your hips sink. The hand of fire leads his ki out horizontally (yoko). This allows your natural weight to ride on top of uke's center.

Here your faith and understanding are tested. Are you able to give up all dependency on physical manipulation and trust completely in the power of one point, the power of the spirit? If you nurture this feeling, eventually you will discover the root of Aikido principle.

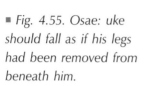
■ *Fig. 4.55. Osae: uke should fall as if his legs had been removed from beneath him.*

You should attempt to bring uke down without disturbing his upper body at all. The upper body is heaven ki and the lower body is earth ki. Following the laws of Heaven and Earth, uke's upper body ki should rise and his lower body ki should sink. Observing the balance of tate and yoko, uke should fall to his rear diagonal as if his legs had been removed from beneath him.

From this position uke can be controlled for as long as necessary, simply by adjusting the focus of your one point and sending his ki out horizontally with your fingertips. If you attempt to hold him by pushing downward, he will easily regain his legs, push up, and escape.

Sending uke's ki outward, do not leave your arm in front of his body where he can grab it and use it to throw you. As uke tries to rise upward, continue to lead his ki out of his body. In order to avoid the atemi he must drop his head and throw his feet forward so that he can escape the strike.

Alternatively, if uke is able to follow you, use a leg sweep at the end of the technique.

■ *Fig. 4.56. Continue to lead uke's ki out of his body.*

■ *Fig. 4.57. Bringing uke down with a leg sweep*

■ *Fig. 4.58. Irimi nage disperses uke's ki through your fingers.*

■ *Fig. 4.59. Entering with tenkan, your opposite hand should grasp from below to ward off an elbow strike.*

Katate Tori Irimi Nage (Kotai)

The basic, or kotai, form of Irimi nage should be practiced from the katate tori, or one-hand grasp attack. When your partner grasps your arm, he is giving you his energy. If you use your mind and kokyu properly, you will hold his entire body with your one point at the moment of contact. The direction of your fingers should automatically continue the direction of uke's ki. The moment uke grasps your arm, his ki is dispersed through your fingers and the ki of your hara enters his center directly.

Entering with tenkan, you may become vulnerable to an elbow strike. In order to prevent this, your opposite hand should grasp from below. In this way you also threaten uke with an elbow strike to his face.

■ Fig. 4.60. Entering with irimi, grasp from above before you pivot.

■ Fig. 4.61. Having entered behind uke, it's logical to expand outward, turning his face away from you.

If you use the irimi approach, grasp from above before you pivot. In this way you will protect your face. The technical differences between the irimi and tenkan versions of Aikido techniques are often overlooked, and the devil, or atemi if you prefer, lies in wait if you overlook the details.

Having entered behind uke, a common mistake is to pull him toward you and place his head against your body. Pulling your partner toward your body for any purpose is to invite his attack. The logical approach to this movement is to expand outward, turning his face away from you.

■ *Fig. 4.62. Katate tori irimi nage*

It may be useful to mention the order of this process once more. First, it is your inside arm that leads uke in the tenkan process (1, 2). Next, your outside arm leads uke out, followed by your inside arm, which expands outward, moving uke away from you (3). As you continue to pour your ki into uke's center, his ki rises upward until he is unbalanced and brought down by your outside arm (4). Next, your inside arm, the hand of water, rides uke down (5). As he rises up and turns into you in order to renew his attack, your outside arm finishes the throw as described above (6).

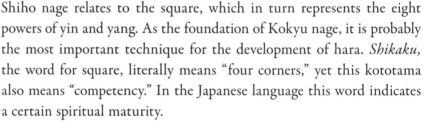

■ *Shiho nage*

THE SPIRIT OF SHIHO NAGE

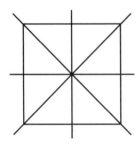

■ *Fig. 4.63. Square with straight lines in all directions*

Shiho nage relates to the square, which in turn represents the eight powers of yin and yang. As the foundation of Kokyu nage, it is probably the most important technique for the development of hara. *Shikaku,* the word for square, literally means "four corners," yet this kototama also means "competency." In the Japanese language this word indicates a certain spiritual maturity.

When the square is seen as an ideogram, or *kanji,* it is pronounced *kakomu,* which means "the boundaries of the universe," the realm of the eight powers of yin and yang. Shikaku is the ability to stand in the center and freely wield the sword of judgment in the eight directions. The Buddhist term for this spiritual authority is *jiyu jizai,* which means "unlimited freedom."

In Shinto ritual the priest waves the sacred wand in the eight directions for the purpose of purification. In Aikido this becomes both sword and barehanded movement.

The study of Shiho nage focuses on the discovery of freedom of mind. Even as your wrists are grasped, how do you send your ki beyond the difficulty? When you are deeply centered in your one point and follow the laws of tate and yoko, the way of freedom is revealed.

■ *Jiyu jizai*

■ *Fig. 4.64. Harai no tachi: waving the sword in the eight directions*

■ *Fig. 4.65. Entering into Ryote tori shiho nage*

Ryote Tori Shiho Nage

Entering

As the basis of Kokyu nage, Shiho nage should be studied, first of all, from the ryote tori, or two-handed grasp attack. The hand of fire leads uke's ki out of his body, while the hand of water sends ki up his arm to control his elbow. Reaching outward to meet uke's attack, draw his ki inward (1). When the power of his attack is fully received in your hara, unification of ki should be complete.

The emphasis is on the vertical direction of uke's arm. Use it as though thrusting with a sword, pushing it toward his elbow and slightly turning to the outside (2). The hand of water is passive. It rests on uke's arm, leading slightly outward but never pushing down. As you keep your arms relaxed and your ki extended, your ki connection can be maintained through concentration alone.

■ *Fig. 4.66. Tai-sabaki: in the matching stance, both people's feet create the form of a parallelogram.*

Fire leads water, yet both are only messengers for the earth ki of hara. Their complementary function is to eliminate uke's resistance so that you can unite directly with his hara. Your hands should never be symmetrical; one is always leading and the other following, or supporting.

Tai-sabaki

At the moment of meeting, the position of both people's feet in the matching, or *ai-hanmi,* stance creates the form of a parallelogram, or a square in motion. Drawing a perpendicular line from your own hara directly into the centerpoint between uke's two feet reveals the path of entering and passing through the technique. As you connect the four corners with a circular form, the forward motion of the parallelogram becomes a spiral, the completed form of Aikido movement.

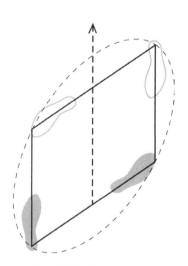

■ *Fig. 4.67. Parallelogram with circle and diagonal*

■ *Fig. 4.68. Use the water mudra to raise uke's ki while you send your ki downward and thrust as with a spear.*

Using the water mudra to raise uke's ki, lower your hanmi and thrust forward beyond the influence of his resistance (1). This is the same hand position you would be using if you were thrusting with a sword or spear. As you send your ki downward and thrust, uke's ki rises up and rides on your center of balance (2). It is much like an ocean wave rolling over a rock.

Do not attempt to lift uke's arms. Pivoting in order to reverse your direction should be a sudden and sharp movement (3). Bring your arms back to your own body as you pivot. Your pivot must be completed before your advancing foot is set down. If weight is placed on your forward foot before you begin to pivot, uke will stop your movement every time.

■ *Fig. 4.69. Pivot to reverse direction with a swift and sharp movement that you complete before your advancing foot is set down.*

■ *Fig. 4.70. Your arms should fall by their own weight as your body rides on top of their free fall.*

Your fingers should seek out the path of least resistance—the path toward freedom. Passing through uke's resistance, your fingers gradually rise up into the fire mudra. As long as your fingers, and therefore your mind, are free, uke will not be able to stop your movement. O-sensei taught, *The tension in your fingers should be equal to the degree of your partner's resistance.*

Tension, in this case, refers to tension of your ki, not your physical muscles or joints. Even as your ki is fully extended, every joint of your hand should be movable.

Nage

Bending from the hips, rather than using your arms in the throw, teaches the use of forward momentum. As in all Aikido techniques, your arms should fall by their own weight as your body rides on top of their free fall (4). Due to your hanmi stance, you should be able to bend sideways and never place your weight on both feet equally.

Shugyo: The Spiritual Training of Technique

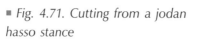
■ *Fig. 4.71. Cutting from a jodan hasso stance*

Throwing in Shiho nage should be practiced with forward momentum, as in cutting from a *jodan hasso* stance. Just as with the sword, throw with an expansive motion, even while gathering ki inside. Mizu no te holds uke's arm, yet it is hi no te that leads the movement. If you attempt to throw with the hand of water, there is a tendency to tighten the shoulders and pull downward. Uke can stop this kind of forceful movement.

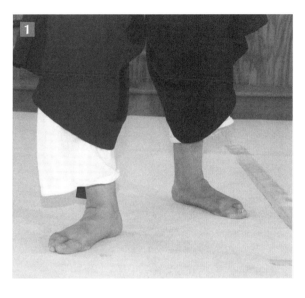
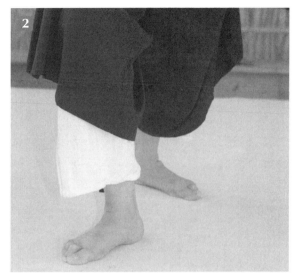

■ *Fig. 4.72. Correct and incorrect placement of feet in the hanmi stance*

Your feet should be angled heel to instep, or at most, heel to heel (1). If your stance is too narrow, heel to toe, you will be unstable sideways (2). If it is wider than heel to heel, you will be unstable in your forward direction (3). The line of throwing should pass between your legs (4).

■ *Fig. 4.73. As you complete the throw, your hara should pull back, preventing uke from pulling you down with him.*

As uke is thrown, the direction of your hara should reverse, thereby pushing your back upward as in a cat stretch. Here again we see the principle of hands and hips working in opposite directions. Finishing with this feeling allows for *zanshin,* or continuing mind, at the end of the throw. This makes it difficult for uke to pull you down with him as he is thrown.

Ura Waza

Before leaving the ryote tori form of Shiho nage, it is necessary to say a little about the differences between the omote and the ura forms. Entering, of course, always begins with omote; yet in the ura form you should stand a good deal taller than in omote. Ura begins with a small hanmi designed for the purpose of pivoting sharply, if necessary.

In the ura form, receive as if preparing to throw with Kokyu nage. Making contact with your handblade, cut down sharply (1). This should unbalance uke and also take you into the ura position behind him (2).

Reaching bottom, your hands meet and lightly close around uke's wrist, much as in a meditation mudra. If you attempt to grasp strongly, uke will be able to stop your motion. Do not attempt to lift here. If you hold loosely and use the water mudra to push through his resistance, he will give way (3).

■ Fig. 4.74. Shiho nage ura

■ Fig. 4.75. The final throw creates a forward-moving spiral.

Perhaps the most common mistake in Shiho nage ura is attempting to extend the arms away from uke's hara. Your arms should stay close to your body as you push backward into his body (see fig. 4.69 on page 201). Drawing uke's ki inward in this way is the same as raising a sword upward into a jodan posture. Once again, the final throw creates a forward-moving spiral as you descend (4).

■ *Fig. 4.76. Emphasize the water mudra when countering uke's shomen uchi attack.*

KOTE GAESHI AND KAITEN NAGE

The basic techniques of Aikido are very few. Truly grasping the essence of Ikkyo, Irimi nage, and Shiho nage, you should be able to apply this understanding easily to all other Aikido techniques. It is, in fact, this ability that determines your degree of understanding.

■ *Fig. 4.77. Change to the fire mudra to control uke's backward movement.*

Katate tori kaiten nage shares many points with Katate tori ikkyo, as does Shomen uchi kote gaeshi with Shomen uchi irimi nage. Kote gaeshi and Kaiten nage, however, strongly reinforce the principle of hand and hip movement and therefore are addressed briefly here.

Shomen Uchi Kote Gaeshi

From a shomen uchi attack, immediately unbalance uke by leading him down with the water mudra. If you emphasize contact with your palm, he will escape easily or even change the technique into a Kaiten nage. If, however, you strongly emphasize the water mudra, you will be able not only to bring him down, but also to restrain him in that position momentarily (1, 2, 3).

Changing to the fire mudra and emphasizing contact with the handblade, control his backward movement (4, 5). Alternating between the use of fire and water ki with mizu no te, and maintaining direct hara-to-hara contact, you should be able to adjust to uke's movement.

■ Fig. 4.78. Kote gaeshi controls uke by alternating between the fire and water mudras and maintaining direct hara-to-hara contact.

Uke, in order to get up safely, must be able to raise your arm without becoming vulnerable to atemi (6). Emphasizing the opposite direction of hands and hips, push uke outward with the water mudra. This is an irimi movement and brings you safely behind him (7).

As your water hand returns to your body, uke is unbalanced by your direct hara connection, not by your arm, as it appears (8). The focus of ki, entering uke's one point from above, makes it impossible for him to rise up and regain his balance. Uke should be unbalanced before you face him. A common mistake here is turning toward uke before beginning the throw. This allows him to regain his balance and leaves you vulnerable to his counterattack.

As uke begins to fall, use the turning of your body to lead him slightly to the outside. The hand of fire makes light contact with uke's fingertips and leads his ki slightly to the outside of his body (9, 10).

Quite frankly, Kote gaeshi is a bad name for this technique. It comes from the older Kote hineri, which literally means "twisting the wrist." There should be no wrist twisting in Aikido. If you control your partner with direct hara-to-hara contact at all times, a slight movement of your one point should be sufficient to bring him down when you decide.

■ *Fig. 4.79. Kote gaeshi: a roundhouse kick to the ribs*

In Aikido, Kote gaeshi is accomplished by leading your partner off balance rather than by turning his wrist strongly to the outside. If you attempt to throw uke by applying pressure to his wrist, he will ignore the pain and use the momentum of your movement to deliver a punch or a roundhouse kick to your ribs.

Tsuki Kaiten Nage

Uke delivers *mune tsuki,* a punch to your midsection. Using the principle of irimi, avoid his punch and bring him forward and off balance with the water mudra. For beginning practice, it is best to sit down on one knee to bring uke off balance (1).

Standing up again, lead uke's ki out of his body with the hand of fire (2). The key point of Kaiten nage is to keep uke continually off balance by leading his ki out of his arm. As you continue this motion, uke is thrown (3, 4).

Never push into uke's body with the hand of fire. To do so allows him to regain his footing and become strong again.

■ *Fig. 4.80. In Tsuki kaiten nage, keep uke off balance by leading his ki out of his arm.*

■ *Fig. 4.81. Incorrect form: pushing into uke's body with the hand of fire allows him to regain his footing.*

5 ■ INOCHI

Aikido as a Spiritual Path

■ *Inochi* 　　人 之 道

Each of us, as our divine birthright, has a direct connection to the absolute. We are each a *bunrei,* or individual part of the great universal spirit. The statement "created in the image of God" means that each of us contains all of the a priori aspects of the great creator spirit of the universe. Just as one cup of water taken out of the ocean is no different from the entire ocean, our soul and spirit are no different from that of the creator spirit of the universe.

In the words of O-sensei, *Ware soku uchu,* or "The universe and I are one and the same." This statement has sometimes been mistranslated to mean, "I am the universe." This is an incorrect rendering of the Japanese original. Such would be the attitude of a fool rather than a saint or wise man. As human beings we are forever uke, the receivers of life.

The seemingly conflicting views of evolution and creationism are not at odds with each other. They are, in fact, two sides of the same coin. We are born from the universal spirit and contain the essence of that perfection. Nevertheless, we must succeed in our own development in order to claim all that our birthright implies.

Universal spirit, being without limitations in either time or space, is necessarily selfless. It has only one function, or purpose: to evolve and manifest its own perfection. The first step in this process is the infinite expansion of A dimension's ki that unceasingly gives birth to and supports all of life. This ki is the actual substance of divine compassion—the consciousness of Su, the creator spirit of the universe.

The universe, as well as our own existence, began with one thought. This is shown in the Japanese word *souzou*. It has the dual meaning of "to create" and "to contemplate." The ki of infinite spirit (*ana*) comes forth in the manifest world as mind (*mana*). Our thoughts, from moment to moment, create and renew the very reality that we perceive. The life will of the universe cannot realize its goal of perfection without human beings. Is there a larger meaning of life than this?

The basic stuff of the universe is consciousness. It is the self-perpetuating force of universal spirit. This abundant compassion (A), meeting itself, creates endless centers (I) from which life forms are born. From these centers, the life will expands outward as the perfect judgment of IE and creates the spiral form underlying all manifestation.

Whether or not the universe is self-conscious is a separate inquiry altogether. It is perhaps the most important question we can ask, yet the answer must be found by each person individually. I put forth my own observations here because they are pertinent to the theme I propose.

Consciousness cannot exist without a body, a medium to carry its vibration. The universal body, however, is infinite. Its center is everywhere and there is no place that it does not fill. This being the case, there is no way to support the illusion of a separate self. Center being everywhere, there is only here and now forever. This is selfless awareness; it is absolute enlightenment, or God-consciousness.

Guided by universal spirit, our own evolution has brought us through the gradual stages of becoming physically upright. Hara, our psychic center, and the "third eye" at the center of our brain are connected vertically, making us antennae for the highest perception—a potentially perfect receiver of universal wisdom.

Realizing this potential, however, requires conscientious practice. It is the destiny of mankind to consciously take part in our own evolution. This practice, *inochi,* is the path of a true human being. It is to follow, and thereby realize, the laws of our own nature. This should be approached physically, psychologically, and spiritually.

Since the physical body contains—and is the basis for—all other dimensions of soul and spirit, in one sense all training is fundamentally physical. "Only the spiritual body, born of inspiration, penetrates all five layers and thus integrates all organs and faculties into one complete whole. . . . Our physical body is not able to penetrate any of the other bodies, yet it is penetrated by all of the other bodies and therefore becomes the natural stage of all spiritual actions and decisions."[1]

Our physical foundation is established mainly through the harmony of our food and our environment. As we are at the top of the animal kingdom, our food should be mainly of vegetable quality. It should go without saying that we should avoid all artificial additives and unnatural chemicals in order to be in tune with nature and our natural environment.

Receiving, the most important part of spiritual development, is best practiced through seated meditation. In addition to our training in technique, we also should include meditation as a part of our daily training. The moving practice of Aikido brings spirit and body together in harmony. We should be clear about the seriousness of our practice, yet never at the expense of joyfulness.

The correct practice of Aikido is more a practice of "how to be" than "how to do." The primary intention of Aikido training is the development of the human potential at all levels, not merely the mastery of technique. If we become overly goal oriented, we miss the essence by looking too much to the outside. When outside and inside are understood as one, there will be no more worry about success or failure. Through purity of practice, our judgment passes through the five levels of *amatsu iwasaka* and we grow in our depth of realization.

Effort alone will not be sufficient in this quest, however. In addition, we need great sincerity and sensitivity. The true nature of human beings has been long since forgotten, and so we flounder about like spiritual beggars, depending on the partial and incomplete teachings of the past. Our physical evolution is basically complete, yet our spiritual growth has hardly even begun. In human beings spiritual evolution must be conscious and intentional.

Inochi, the path of a human being, requires returning to U dimension, the ground of being, and revealing the contents of our original mind. Using that as a foundation, we are then able to progress step by step through the other dimensions (OAE) and approach the ultimate wisdom of I dimension, the life will itself. "Will is not an activity of the mind, but of self."[2]

As our judgment and clarity evolve, gradually we are released from our conditioning. We spend less time in the past and the future, and more time in being here and now. In the words of O-sensei, *Cast off limiting thoughts and return to true emptiness. Stand in the midst of the great void. This is the secret of the warrior's path.*

When we finally stand in the place of E dimension's clarity, we see that sensual, emotional, and even ideological fulfillment occurs only within our own center of consciousness and that each level of consciousness serves not only for the realization of the next, but also for the maintenance of a balanced and healthy view of life. Rather than trying to get rid of our karma, conditioning, or basic desires, we are better served to focus our efforts on the unveiling of our truly human qualities.

Having the good fortune to be born as human beings, it is a shame to waste our time. That which ceases to progress is already in a state of degeneration. The inability to deal with change is the hallmark of the ego. It can't survive in an environment of impermanence, any more than real freedom and joy can continue without adaptability.

At this time in our history and evolution, the choice of whether or not to undertake this most important of all pursuits is no longer optional. It is no longer an extracurricular activity. Our efforts now, or the lack of them, will determine our own future and that of our descendants.

As we let go of attachment to success of any kind, including that of spiritual development, we must begin to practice the truth of our life. The partial and symbolic teachings of the past will no longer keep the destructive momentum of our present society at bay. Our present society is held together mainly by the rigidity and forcefulness of law.

The time of the Buddha is over. It is time for the complete manifestation of divine spirit. The universal spirit is no longer hidden. The age of the perfection of one spirit, four souls, three origins, and eight powers is here. In a word, the great yang ki of the spiritual world is now becoming manifest.

Human judgment has long since ceased to play a part in human affairs. Justice can never be produced by majority rule. It is nothing but violence against the minority. When order can no longer be maintained through force, we will fall into chaos.

As long as we remain stuck in the dualistic view of self and other, we are destined to experience suffering and disappointment. As we get beyond the illusion of a separate self, it becomes possible to enjoy our lives fully. When freedom is understood as having only one choice—that which must be done—we become stuck with it. This is truly good fortune.

Fortunately, following the path of a human being is also the greatest enjoyment we can experience. The path of Aikido, as created and practiced by Morihe Ueshibai O-sensei, is much more than a martial art. To accomplish it requires contemplation, physical training, sincerity of purpose, and a huge appetite for freedom and happiness.

The path of Aikido originates in the original teachings of Shinto. This is a Mahayana, or macro, approach. It concerns itself directly with the improvement of society and the human condition. This path was described by the ancient emperor Amaterasu Oh Mi Kami as an eightfold path, a means toward the creation of a society of health, peace, and prosperity.

The first step (Hi) is to research the natural world and gather knowledge. It is to familiarize yourself with the various approaches seeking to understand the truth of life. We should attempt to understand past, present, and future through the truth of history, modern science, and the various spiritual disciplines.

This was also the attitude of the founder. *Striking an accord between modern science and ancient Budo beliefs is the great path that is our goal. I would like to realize the great essence of Budo thought, this spirit of accord between the old and the new.*

The second step (Ti) is to refine our knowledge through contemplation until it can be understood as the working of one principle. The third step is to intuitively grasp *makoto,* the mind of sincerity (Si), as our own. As we uncover this mind, it becomes clear that the problems of the world are all based on our own false view of reality.

When we become clear about the fundamental unity of things, our

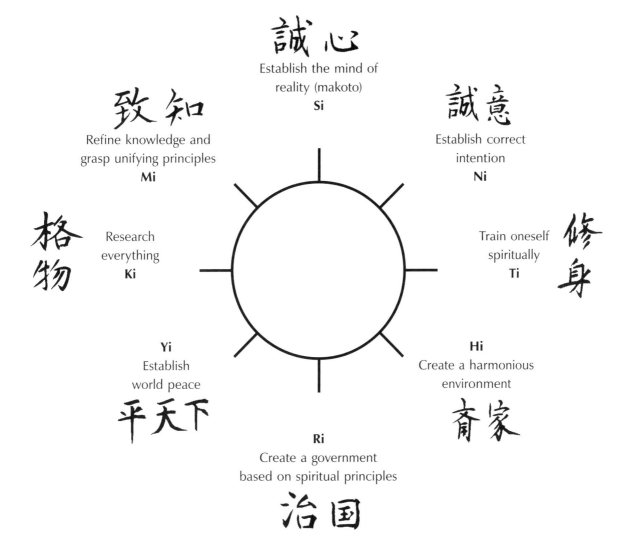

誠心
Establish the mind of
reality (makoto)
Si

致知
Refine knowledge and
grasp unifying principles
Mi

誠意
Establish correct
intention
Ni

格物
Research
everything
Ki

修身
Train oneself
spiritually
Ti

Yi
Establish
world peace

平天下

Hi
Create a harmonious
environment

斉家

Ri
Create a government
based on spiritual principles

治国

■ *Fig. 5.1. The eight
powers of Amaterasu Oh
Mi Kami*

direction also should become crystal clear. There is no longer room for even the slightest deviation from the way. In the words of the founder, *Man, as a division of the great universal spirit, should already know what it is that he must do.*

Gaining clarity of intention (Ki) we begin *shugyo,* the training of body and spirit (Mi). It is necessary to embody the truth before it can be properly shared with anyone else. This is not a conceptual process; it must be based on realization through actual experience.

As the levels of self-protection and delusion are peeled back one by

**Inochi: Aikido as
a Spiritual Path**

one, it becomes clear that there is no enemy, no one to protect or even to save. Our former states of unrest, fear, and longing are replaced by compassion for others and a sense of peace in ourselves. This must first be realized within our daily life (Ri). Only then can it become a positive influence in the lives of others (Yi).

This is the path of a human being. It is to protect and nurture all life on this planet (Ni), now and for the generations to come. There is no pot of gold at the end of the rainbow—no greatness, no rewards, nothing to seek, and nothing to be gained. To discover the path of a human being is to realize our own nature and manifest it in the world.

O-sensei was perfectly clear in expressing the meaning of Aikido training, so why should people today think otherwise? *The realization of our true substance and potential is the purpose of creation. The realization of divine love, the universal consciousness, is our responsibility to the creator. Aikido is the principle and the path that join humanity with the universal consciousness.*

MECHANICAL JUDGMENT: REALM OF THE INSENTIENT

The process of our evolution has taken us from a single cell to our present state as human beings. In that process we have passed through the entire history of life on this planet. From the moment of conception leading up to our physical birth we review that entire process once again. The final step, realization of our true nature, requires us to intentionally seek out that experience one more time.

At the time of our birth, we begin with the consciousness of U dimension, the realm of the insentient. This is the mechanical, or automatic, level of judgment. Regardless of its lack of self-realization, it flawlessly manages the movement of nature and the cosmos. This is because it manifests perfect receiving. It is the perfect uke, and therefore delivers the perfect response to all situations. This is the defining characteristic of the enlightened mind, yet the insentient utters not a single word and teaches by example alone.

The difference between the mind of the insentient and the enlightened mind is perhaps only that of self-consciousness. It is much like the analogy of a newborn baby compared to a wise old man. Although they share many characteristics, their wisdom and experience are worlds apart. As a newborn baby we begin with U dimension's consciousness, yet at the center of that dark world is I dimension, the source of wisdom and realization.

In the realm of the insentient, I dimension's wisdom goes unrealized, yet it is essential for the creation of the earth and especially the mineral world. The straight lines of I dimension's ki are especially strong in the minerals of the earth and in precious stones such as diamonds and crystals.

In human beings, the mineral world governs our nervous system and regulates the quality of our blood. Our mental health depends largely on the many trace minerals in our bodies. It is, in fact, the iron in our blood that makes sound judgment possible. A lack of iron leads to loss of memory and distorted judgment.

In the vegetable kingdom, we find the intense ki of I dimension in cereal grains reaching straight upward toward the heavens. When they become full with ripeness, they humbly bow their heads and offer themselves as the staple food for the development of humankind. Here again we see the perfect teaching of the insentient.

As in human beings, the insentient also contains the five dimensions of life's ki. The forms of nature embody the ki of universal wisdom for those who have eyes and ears to hear and see it. The entire consciousness of *itsura,* the fifty sounds, is present, yet until the physical form evolves sufficiently, it cannot be realized. If the vibration for the color red were not present in your physical brain, you would not be able to see it in a rose.

Due to the expansive ki of A dimension, the vegetable world has incredible durability and strength combined with marvelous adaptability. It is a shame, yet even human beings often fall short of the adaptability of the vegetable kingdom. Human beings, like the vegetable world, should pass naturally through the five stages of development and reach the maturity of self-realization. The very consciousness that created us continually replenishes our life for this very purpose.

Why, then, is it so difficult for us to realize success in this way? To do so would be to accept the demise of the ego, our sense of a separate self. The ego will never surrender to its own extinction without a fight. Refusing to take on our real, one and only enemy, we allow the ego to become stronger, and our conditioning becomes deeper day by day. Eventually the opportunity of realization is lost.

There is no particular path that inevitably leads to realization. "The methods themselves do not transform. It is the dedication and sincerity of the individual that accounts for the possibility of realization. All methods are merely activities performed while waiting for divine presence to make itself known to you; to make you receptive to the divine."[3]

All paths are methods designed to self-destruct once they have served their purpose. The most important factor in Aikido, or any other path, is therefore *makoto,* or sincerity. Unless we are clear about our reasons for practice and serious about wanting to change, we will be unable to succeed.

FIRST THREE INSTINCTS: THE ANIMAL WORLD

Within the vegetable and mineral realms of nature, consciousness is mainly mechanical. U dimension creates the five senses yet functions from mechanical judgment alone. A dimension coming forth as Wa, or individual self, utilizes these senses to manifest sensory priorities, escaping from what is unpleasant and gravitating toward that which is pleasing.

The realm of emotions, however, for all practical purposes probably begins with the animal kingdom, or *moving things,* as they are called in Japanese. In the animal kingdom, O dimension's ki activates the small brain, simultaneously giving birth to both instinct and independent movement. Our nourishment still comes from the earth, yet our intestine, the root through which we receive it, is now carried with us.

Instinct is the primitive state of memory. This is an enormous leap in evolution; it lays the foundation for human consciousness. Each level of consciousness becomes the foundation for that which follows.

U dimension's mechanical judgment gives birth to the sensory realm A. A dimension's expanding awareness, in turn, is given continuity by instinct and memory, the concentrating power of O dimension.

Resulting from this momentous leap, the animal kingdom manifests the consciousness of UAO as the first three instincts—the desire for food, sex, and emotional fulfillment. Food and sex are strictly physical, yet the instinct of giving birth and caring for the young, although essential for the continuation of the species, also creates emotional fulfillment, a caring for something outside of one's self.

Before addressing the fourth level of consciousness, it may by useful to backtrack and see this same process of UAO in the dawning of human consciousness. The first step is standing in the void from which self-consciousness was born. It is from this place that our self-awareness began. The dawning of this awareness (A-Wa) is recorded in Christian mythology as our "leaving the garden of Eden."

BIRTH OF THE ISLANDS: THE POTENTIAL OF HIGHER JUDGMENT

Before formalized religion, the birth and evolution of consciousness was recorded symbolically in mythological tales of creation. As material society progressed and people became less intuitive, the original meaning of these stories was lost and they came to be taken literally, rather than as metaphorical examples of human evolution. The Old Testament Book of Genesis and the Japanese Kojiki, or record of ancient events, are two examples.

In the Kojiki, the story of creation is explained metaphorically through the birth of deities, and subsequently through the birth of islands, the space within which these deities reside. The first seventeen deities are the pre-conditional, or a priori, aspects of mental vibration. These are described in chapter 1 as the levels of amatsu iwasaka, the foundation of the human spiritual condition.

As we saw in chapter 1, the establishment of the seventeen deities is the gradual stabilization of the life will and power, the axis of the spiral of creation. The last two deities to be established are Izanagi and Izanami. Manifesting the centripetal force of solar winds and the

■ *Fig. 5.2. Onokoro Shima: the island of self-creation*

centrifugal force of the earth spinning on its axis, the human spiritual form is created. The field of ki in which this occurs is our own consciousness. It is the womb of Su. It is referred to in the Kojiki as Onokoro Shima, the island of self-creation.*

Onokoro Shima: The Island of Self-Creation

As described in chapter 2, the cycling and blending of vertical (tate) and horizontal (yoko) energies creates the first spiritual form. The mythological expression of this blending is illustrated as the two deities, Izanagi and Izanami, thrusting a spear, *ame no nuhoko,* down from Heaven and into the brine of the ocean. This ocean is the ground of being, and it is our physical body. In other words, it is the kototama of Su-U.

Nuhoko, the spear, symbolizes the tongue through which we manifest words. The individual kototama show the meaning in detail. Nu is the materialization of No, the descending of instinctive mind from the kototama of Su. Ho is the fullness of creative ki, which begins the process of creation by dividing the world into subject and object. Ko is cycling and contracting ki, the materialization of spirit. In other words, the life will and power unifying body and mind create the first spark of instinct, or *honno.*

This is the activity that takes place on the island called Onokoro Shima, the island of Su. *Shima,* or island, is the enclosure of our own heart and mind. It is our first ability to unite feeling and sound, to express ourselves. It also means *shimeru,* to be soaked or totally drenched—to the point where there is no separation—with intimacy. We are so immersed in the reality of our own spirit that we are totally unaware of it.

Ono is self, and *koro,* once again, is ki revolving and materializing. The quality of Su is called *kanro no hou,* the sweet nectar of heavenly dew. This is the spiritual ki that descends into our brain as consciousness. It is the life ki within which we are totally soaked or immersed.

---

*In Japanese, some letters have more than one pronunciation. The letter for *k* sounds like *g* when it appears in the middle of a word, and *sh* becomes *j* when used in a phrase. Therefore, the word *onokoro* may sometimes appear as *onogoro* and the word *shima,* or island, may appear as *jima* in some contexts.

In a word, Onokoro Shima is our own body and mind, the meeting place of time, space, and dimension. Without these three factors nothing can manifest. It is our own perception, occurring here and now, that makes the world appear. When the dimensions of spirit and the original rhythms of nature are combined, the relative world appears. To imagine the physical world existing outside of consciousness is to miss its intrinsic nature.

The process of manifesting consciousness as reality happens in three stages. The first is called *ana,* the name of Heaven. As explained in chapter 1, this is the seventeen a priori deities of amatsu iwasaka. Ana is the spiritual realm of feeling before word consciousness. When this consciousness descends into our brain as thought it becomes mana, the realm of thought.

■ *Ana*

Inochi: Aikido as a Spiritual Path

223

■ *Mana*

■ *Kana*

The literal translation of *mana,* or *manna* as it is pronounced in the Bible, is "the true word." Mana can be spoken only by the pure and enlightened mind. It occurs when there is not one iota of difference among one's words, feelings, and actions. At this time the vibration of the words spoken mesh perfectly with the objective reality that they describe. When a human being speaks the true word it can have far-reaching power and influence.

After ana and mana comes the third stage of consciousness. It is called *kana,* "the name of God." This is creative consciousness. It is the manifestation of thought as form, letters, or visual words. From the *Kototama Hissho: In ancient times the shapes and forms created by the ki of fire and water were understood as katakana, "the names of the gods." Over time, the idea of spiritual ki creating the form of nature was forgotten. To our modern mentality, such an idea sounds preposterous, yet this is the foundation of the philosophy of the Far East.*

In Shinto, the idea of creating the forms of nature out of conscious intent is referred to as *kami waza,* or divine technique. This phrase was sometimes used to describe the techniques of O-sensei's Aikido as well. Both are an attempt to perfectly blend the ki of our own spirit and soul with the creator spirit of the universe.

Even our thoughts (mana) and feelings (ana) alter the quality of our own and other people's lives. This influence is greatly increased when these thoughts and feeling are brought into form as speech and action. Our individual karma and the karma of our world both begin with the activity of our mouth. It is through food and words, the physical and the spiritual, that the wheel of manifestation is turned. This karma begins with the birth of Awaji no Ho no Sawake Shima, the second island.

Awaji no Ho no Sawake Shima: The Island of Self-Consciousness

Awaji no Ho no Sawake Shima is the opening of the womb of Su. It is the first activity that takes place within Onokoro Shima. At the intersection of Heaven and Earth's force (I-Wi), the ripeness of ki comes forth as Ho, the creative breath of Heaven. It is likened to the ripe fruit of cereal grain. Like the point of a spearhead, it divides the womb of Su.

The fire ki of Ho descends into the ground of being (Su-U) and

divides the world into O and Wo, or subject and object. As mentioned above, this activity is the realm of instinctive mind, yet it is our own mechanical judgment (We) that decides the moment when this awareness begins. This is the place where the activity of creation takes place within our own hara, yet we are unaware of it.

Sa means "a subtle difference" or "a slight difference," and *wake* means "to separate" or "to divide." In other words, *sawake* is the subtle difference, or distinction, between what is seen as self and other. The instinctive mind of O dimension cannot clearly perceive this difference.

Following the kototama of Ho, the breath of Heaven comes forth as He, Hu, Hi, and Ha, each one expanding to the right and to the left and giving birth to the dimensions of subjective and objective consciousness. In this way the word soul of Ha, the power of recognition, gives birth to

A and Wa, the sense of self and other. In other words, A sees itself, the reflection of our own mind, and interprets it as Wa, or objective reality.

The *ji* of Awaji means *michi,* the path toward realization. The opening of A-Wa, or awareness, is the beginning of our journey as human beings. Beginning with U dimension, the ground of being, we must pass through the dimensions of AOE and finally reach the perfection of wisdom in I dimension. Lacking this, we lose touch with the forces of nature and our lives remain unfulfilled.

■ *Fig. 5.5. Iyo, the space of a human being*

Iyo no Futana Shima: The Island of Humanity

With Awaji no Ho no Sawake Shima, we saw the separation of Heaven and Earth, the advent of individual awareness. This expansive movement, however, has no root and, therefore, no means to realize itself. Standing in between and reuniting Heaven and Earth, we manifest the life will, our human essence. This is the activity of Iyo no Futana Shima. *Iyo* means "to unite the breath" and *futana* means "two names."

Heaven and Earth, subject and object being originally the same, are attracted to each other and reunite in the space of Iyo no Futana Island. This is also called *ningen,* the space of a human being. The polarity of A and Wa is united by a common center, the kototama of Ya. As mentioned in chapter 1, this is called "the opening of the eye of Heaven," nature becoming conscious of itself.

In this way the unifying power of human beings unfolds on the island of Iyo no Futana. The in breath of Yi is born from the attraction of I and Wi, the life will and power. The life will creates our life power, or force, in order to manifest itself. This is Wi, the centripetal power at the center of our hara. To the degree that this ki is strong, it produces the potential for a healthy and long life.

The attraction between the water ki of U and the fire ki of Wu produces Yu, the perfect harmony of fire and water. E and We together produce Ye, the perfectly balanced judgment that unifies all things. O and Wo combined produce Yo, which stabilizes the world by standing in between subjective and objective mind.

In this way we can see that the essence of human beings is created by Heaven and Earth, yet it is mankind that unifies the ki of fire and water, the activity of the relative world in which we live. This is the destiny of human beings; it is the goal that we walk toward, yet it can't be accomplished until we are fully aware of our own potential and consequent responsibility.

The clarity and expression of our judgment depend on our ability to surrender our physical tension and receive the power of Heaven and Earth without resistance. The form and feeling of our Aikido technique is a barometer of how well we succeed in doing this. As individuals, we do not create our own life, yet we are given the responsibility of deciding how to manage it. How we manifest the power that comes to us is our own decision. That decision ultimately decides the quality of our lives.

Standing between and unifying Heaven and Earth, yet unaware of our own significance, we begin our solitary journey home. As with the animal kingdom, we possess the first three instincts to ensure our survival and continuance, yet also like other animals, our entire consciousness at this stage exists only to satisfy that basic world of physical and emotional desire. In other words, we see from the point of view of Wa Wi Wu We Wo.

INOCHI:
THE PATH OF A HUMAN BEING

Human beings, whether we accept it or not, are just one more product of nature. We sometimes imagine ourselves to be outside of it, yet we never really could be. As for the rest of nature, both sentient and insentient, it has prepared a path for us to grow into, and to do so is our ultimate fulfillment. The path, which is inscribed on our spirit and our DNA, is the realization of our own nature.

"When fish move through the water, however they move, there is no end to the water. When birds fly through the sky, however they fly, there is no end to the sky."[4] In this same way we also are swimming and flying in a sea of word consciousness. Endowed with the abstract ability of word consciousness, our E dimension's judgment becomes creative thought. We no longer simply observe the world but consciously create it.

As a result, the experience of awakening is much more traumatic and profound for us than it is for the rest of the animal kingdom. When the womb of U dimension's consciousness opens up into A and Wa, the distinction between self and other has implications that extend much further. The perception of self and other becomes an abstract idea. We begin to contemplate our own vulnerability and insecurity.

When we first experience awareness (A-Wa-Re), we cannot see that it is our own capacity for judgment that creates the separation of self and other, subject and object. In the New Testament we find, "And the light shineth in the darkness; and the darkness comprehended it not."[5] The initial light of recognition (A) expands and is continued through our memory capacity (O). Unfortunately, coming from the objective limitations of Wa, we still can't recognize it as the light of our own subjective consciousness.

The kototama of A, therefore, has the meaning of *ware,* or divided self. A dimension's ki gives us awareness and spiritual feeling, yet it is also the beginning of duality, ignorance, and suffering. It is the beginning of our spiritual path, yet in religious symbolism it is sometimes called *akuma,* or the space of evil or the devil.

The difference between the physical view based on U dimension's ki and that based on A dimension's ki was explained technically in chapter 4, yet it is useful, if not absolutely necessary here, to explain these opposing views from a spiritual and psychological point of view.

The strictly physical perspective of AIUEO is the kanagi order of development. U dimension's physical consciousness cannot understand or even see the higher realm of AI, which is pure wisdom and compassion. Our physical base, therefore, becomes the criterion for all of our activity. Developing in the order of UEO, our physical experience is judged by our intellect and then remembered as a reference for future judgments.

U dimension's perspective is stuck in the world of appearances. Seeing the world as fundamentally physical, neither the spiritual feeling of A dimension nor the wisdom of I dimension can be understood. The advent of our awareness is shadowed and unclear.

With our judgment (E) functioning strictly in the service of our physical perspective (U), we seek to discern reality through knowledge. We compare and judge the value of each thing, one by one, throwing out what is useless and preserving that which seems to further our purpose. Memory is used as a basis for future judgments and is consciously edited when it doesn't mesh comfortably with our idea of how things should be.

Depending on intellect, we endeavor to justify our view of life. If we perceive the material world as basic reality, we seek knowledge to support that view. This is kanagi, the way of science. If, on the other hand, we view the invisible world as the basic reality, we seek out knowledge to support *that* view. This is the order of AOUE, the sugaso stage that creates a religious approach to inquiry.

The sugaso order is based on the continual expansion of A dimension's ki. "A dimension is not limited to time and space; it moves freely. For this reason the subjective self (A) separates from the spiritual phenomena of Wa, and universal phenomena is seen as the existence of God."[6]

A dimension is the source of our spiritual feeling and inspiration, yet its infinitely expanding nature is inaccessible. The human mind recoils at the idea of the infinite, yet the sugaso approach is unable to turn the light around and look inside for the source. This refusal to acknowledge the responsibility of human freedom results in a vague kind of spirituality, the contents of which cannot be verified.

Coming from the feeling of A dimension, the strictly material view of U dimension's perspective appears foolish. U dimension's perspective, on the other hand, sees the view of A as a convenient fantasy with no basis in reality. Neither side can see that the separation is created by its own limited perception, and both sides, therefore, continue to be dualistic. "The sense of A as *I am,* acting in unlimited and timeless space without dimension, can never be reconciled with U dimension's physical sense of self."[7]

As in the rest of the animal kingdom, A dimension manifests our sensory judgment—seeking pleasure and attempting to avoid pain. Our O dimension, retaining this experience, produces emotional sensibilities beginning with likes and dislikes. It also allows for the retention of experience as knowledge, and therefore intellectual judgment.

E dimension gives us the potential for creative thought, yet until we actually are coming from that place, its only use is to reinforce the dualistic perspective of either U or A dimension. It is still our E dimension's judgment that decides the method and direction that we use to achieve our goals, yet it can never withstand the test of daily life until it is based on what actually exists (I).

Human beings are not limited, however, to either the realm of the senses or the limitations of speculation. We are born with the capacity to realize all five dimensions of our being. The retention of experience becomes the basis of abstract concepts, which, in turn, give birth to a fourth instinct, the desire for knowledge and understanding. It is only this relentless desire that can lead us to the truth of unity.

In spite of the chaos and suffering that our abstract potential has brought into the world, it is still the only tool through which we can unravel our own delusion. Our judgment creates the original separation—our exit from paradise. The ability to reflect on our own thought processes creates a degree of freedom that we have not yet learned to handle wisely, or even safely. Our desire for knowledge has led us to a scientifically advanced society; at the same time, our spiritual development has been almost completely obscured.

This is an unfortunate reality. Very few, if any, of our leaders approach their elevated positions from a place of higher judgment. More often, their motivation is greed for wealth and power. Someone who doesn't see the result of actions beyond his or her own lifetime can hardly lead others toward a peaceful society.

There comes a point where we must recognize that our own faulty perception is the source of the problem. The sum of the parts will never equal the whole, and intellect, which is inherently dualistic, cannot grasp reality. On the contrary, when intellect is our highest reference point, it tends to isolate us further from others.

Following the way of strict materialism, or "might makes right," is blind and leads to a short and relatively meaningless existence. This is the way of UEO, the order of kanagi. Seeking to grasp reality through the spirit as a separate entity, we are forever adrift in a vague and irresolvable dilemma. This is the sugaso order of AOUE.

This spirituality of sugaso separates itself from all other views and also from the physical side of reality. This is cutting off the source of real spiritual growth. We can never truly grasp anything without physical experience. Both sides being dualistic, neither can discover the wisdom of unity.

In the end it is only the path of unity—the path of wisdom—that leads to a balanced and totally sane approach to life. This is the futonorito order of AIEOU. It is based on the perfect wisdom of IE. It is the unity of Heaven (AI), man (IE), and Earth (OU). This order also may be expressed as AEIOU.

Futonorito is the expression of complete freedom and responsibility —the enlightened mind. From the sugaso point of view, the creative independence of futonorito is a frightening and dangerous perspective. However, to the free man coming from the judgment of IE, the sugaso approach to spirituality is seen as somewhat childish. The charts of the amatsu kanagi, amatsu sugaso, and amatsu futonorito orders on pages 30–32 should be used to clarify these psychological aspects as well.

RETURNING TO THE ORIGIN

Up to this point we have seen the four dimensions of AOUE in the service of separatism, a world-view of self and other, and survival of the fittest. Both the strictly material view of kanagi and the philosophical-religious view of sugaso are, in the final analysis, materialistic. It is for this reason that the sugaso view ends up creating God in the image of man.

This dualism is the true meaning of ignorance, and in its extreme it becomes full-blown arrogance, the root cause of violence and suffering throughout our human history. When we open our minds to the reality of dynamic monism, it becomes impossible to continue this kind of activity. When we realize that all of the problems of the world are the result of our own mistaken judgment, it becomes possible to reverse this direction.

Born into human form, our true nature cannot be suppressed indefinitely. More and more people today are reaching a point of extreme discontent. Something is missing; something is fundamentally wrong and the problem is not limited to any one individual. We must go beyond the intellect and begin to see not only the fundamental unity of all things, but also that all human beings are one family and have but one origin.

When our mutual dependence is understood, it gives us a more practical and realistic sense of morality. Real morality is the product of higher judgment, not lofty or restrictive teachings. When we really begin to function from the higher levels of our E dimension's capacity, the lower levels of judgment are subjugated and brought under control.

There is no need, therefore, to eliminate our sensory or emotional sensibilities. The golden rule of "Do unto others as you would have them do unto you" is all the morality we would ever need, if we truly loved our fellow man. Attempting to impose morality through rules is an infantile mentality that is unable to accept personal responsibility. It is an insult to, and violence against, human judgment.

With the birth of social judgment we begin to understand the universality of personal experience. As creatures of conditioning, we share the human condition, and each of us must deal with it directly. No amount of knowledge will bring peace to our mind. It is time, once again, to return to our spiritual birthplace, the island of Onokoro Shima, and clarify the contents of our own life ki.

In the words of Aikido master Zenzaburo Akazawa, "O-sensei was an astonishing person, that's for sure. However, without doing some kind of spiritual training, no one can ever hope to become like him. People who are training today may well be folding their hands before the Kamisama, but few are practicing Zazen. They cannot hope to become divinely inspired as O-sensei did."[8]

The Zen proverb, "In the beginning rivers and trees are just rivers and trees," shows the starting place. We begin with the body, the physical world. Turning the light of our E dimension inside and sinking deeply into our own center, our mind ceases to wander and we merge with the kototama of Su. This degree of stillness can't be obtained easily in movement; first it should be found in silent meditation.

Imagine the world without you in it. Getting ourselves out of the picture is a good deal more comfortable than you might imagine, and it results in a much greater sense of clarity. At the most fundamental level of one spirit, four souls, we are all basically the same.

There is the obvious side of our existence—the person we call by our first name and all of the conditioned traits and characteristics that we identify with that person. Seen in terms of tate and yoko, it is yoko, the self that we define in terms of the space that we occupy. It is the side of our self that divides one thing from another and weighs our own relative value against the things around us.

Tate, on the other hand, is the temporal self that lives within our relative personality yet stands aside from it. This is the self that exists only in the present moment in *nakaima,* the absolute here and now. It is perception itself.

The first object of *naikan,* or silent meditation, is to stand outside of the mental activities of our everyday monkey mind and impartially observe them. Gradually, from this perspective we are able to realize the impersonal nature of our apparent self. Within U dimension, all other dimensions of our soul and spirit are revealed one by one until we begin to uncover I dimension, the essence of being. This requires the cessation of ego and the discovery of a radical kind of faith in life itself.

The ultimate goal of Aikido, and all other spiritual disciplines, is to intuitively grasp real faith, to hold it in your own hara, and to live from that place. When this happens the world is no longer seen as a threat, and your ego-based desires are subjugated by your aspirations for the health, peace, and prosperity of others.

To take a phrase from the Tao Te Ching, "Effect emptiness to the extreme, guard stillness carefully; as myriad things act in concert, I watch the return."[9] In other words, allowing things to be as they are, we dwell in the emptiness of U dimension's ki until the original yang ki of A dimension's spiritual quality reveals itself. "Watching the return" is not a passive activity; it requires great diligence and one-pointed concentration.

The first important awareness is awareness of the body. Our own body, as well as that of the universe, is a body of ki, or spiritual energy. Immersed in the ki of Su-U-Mu, we come to see the unity that has always been there. As long as we continue to divide between our physical body and the world of spirit, the real nature of life will continue to evade us.

As we persevere in our concentration, awareness of our physical body gradually fades away and the struggle subsides. Continuing still further, eventually nothing remains but the breath of the universe. The emptiness of the material world is not really empty at all. It is the breath—the fullness of ki. "Emptiness is the universe itself, the real existence, before the appearance of phenomenon."[10] Understanding ki as the basic reality, the separation between self and other becomes very difficult to support.

"The fact, once considered as a vague dream or a meaningless delusion, turns out to be the real fact itself. Why, because the origin and

有難い

■ *Arigatai, "gratitude"*

cause of the things considered as dreams and delusion has now become clear."[11] At this time it is said that *Rivers and trees are no longer rivers and trees.*

The light of A dimension's spiritual feeling shines through and illuminates the world of appearances. "I now am not it; it now is me."[12] There is no separate self to protect or save. We are living within the womb of life itself. There is no real separation, yet there is always order in real events.

It is our own mind that illuminates the world, yet as human beings we are always uke, the receiver of life. With this realization the real quality of our A dimension's ki reveals itself. It comes forth abundantly as light and warmth. It is the light of truth (Wa) and the overflowing warmth of selfless compassion (A). It is this light that, in the words of Zen master Hakuin, "shatters the discriminating mind to reveal the awakened essence." This is the light that is called "the formless field of benefaction"; it is endless and unconditional giving that never can be repaid. It contains not one iota of negativity. Merging with this all embracing ki is *arigatai,* a deep feeling of gratitude.

In practicing this we maintain beginner's mind—the place from which we automatically seek to nurture and protect. On the mat as well, our emphasis should be not on power, but rather on nurturing a large and magnanimous feeling toward everyone. One who embodies the virtue of A dimension's ki accepts the difficulties of daily life as an opportunity for personal growth and development and accepts them with gratitude.

■ *Natsukashisa, "nostalgia"*

When we practice compassion in daily life, we nurture the spiritual virtue of O dimension. In Shinto it is called *natsukashisa,* or nostalgia. This is not the usual longing for, or sugarcoating of, the past. Rather it is an insight into the timelessness of the present. In this very moment is past, present, and future, and all that we perceive is nothing other than

Inochi: Aikido as a Spiritual Path

235

our own nature. Nothing is omitted or taken for granted; the mundane itself is the divine manifestation.

The meaning of this *natsukashisa* is closer to the Japanese word *satori,* or spiritual awakening. The kototama of Sa Tori may be interpreted as "to remove the difference," or conversely, "to remember the original unity." All things are seen as equally sacred, therefore there is nothing holy or even special. It is a remembering of a perfection and spirituality that has never, even for an instant, been lost.

In Taoist philosophy it is portrayed with the image of the wise old man who has never left his own small village yet understands the mysteries of the world. Walking the same old paths over a lifetime, how intimately we merge, blend, and even become them. In the Japanese fine arts it is called *wabi sabi,* the essence of timeless antiquity manifest here and now.

■ *Uruwashisa, "elegance"*

Continuing to develop our judgment through daily training, meditation, and introspection, we begin to see the intelligence and elegance of divine design. All antagonisms are seen to be complementary. We see that the beauty and gracefulness of nature lie in its economy, simplicity, and effectiveness. In Shinto, it is called *uruwashisa,* which means "grace" or "elegance." This is the spiritual quality of E dimension's ki. It is the kototama of Re merging with I dimension to become Rei.

To bring this feeling into our own body and mind is to see the world through the eyes of ideological judgment. It is to practice the mind of the sage, or Bodhisattva. It is here that the principle of nature's harmony becomes clear and practical. This clarity of judgment reveals the way of changing adversity into benefit. Walking directly into the hearts of others and changing discord into harmony—this is the real meaning of *irimi-tenkan.*

It is to change sickness into health, dependency into true faith, and ultimately war into peace, all without opposing others or employing forceful methods. The greater the challenge, the greater should be the joy in undertaking it. This requires the development of a deeply yang ki, a completely positive attitude.

It is the judgment capacity of E dimension's ki that controls and maintains the dynamic balance of the eight powers, the real events of everyday life. It is only through this constant judgment that proper balance is possible. When the eight powers are balanced, we become rooted in the space of a human being between Heaven and Earth, in the kototama of I and Wi. The life will is our root in wisdom, and the life power is our root in this physical world.

Beginning with A dimension, each subsequent dimension's ki is more yang and intense. This increasing intensity is the development of a more intuitive and fine-tuned perception. As our E dimension becomes more intense, it becomes the power of subtle differentiation within unity or oneness. In Zen teachings our intuitive judgment is called "the means of crossing the river when the bridge is out" or "finding your way at night without a lantern." In the end, this is the only thing we can depend on.

Coming from E dimension we naturally pursue our daily life as the highest art form. If we live our life as a way to pass time, this kind of refinement is impossible. When we are free of attachment to that which does not, in the long run, create a better world, our influence reaches far beyond our original intentions.

As our judgment becomes more refined, we sink deeply into the experience of the present moment; less and less time is spent dwelling in either the past or the future. This practice of seeing unity from moment to moment is studying the ki of I dimension. When we are standing in the moment and using our judgment to unify all antagonisms, we are practicing the perfect judgment of amatsu futonorito, the natural order of mind.

Amatsu futonorito begins with AI, divine wisdom and compassion. Neither of these can exist separately. Pure love must be completely impersonal, and this depends on the wisdom of I dimension. On the other hand, wisdom would have no way of expressing itself without compassion. When these are established together they are the ki of universal harmony.

When our judgment comes from AI, it is expressed as IE, perfect receiving and, therefore, a perfect response. In Buddhism it is called "unity attained." Zen master Dogen spoke of it, saying, "The Blue Mountains are neither sentient nor insentient. The self is neither sentient nor insentient."[13] It can't be pinned down or compared to anything; it is simply existence.

Bringing the result of that judgment to fruition is the kototama of

Inochi: Aikido as
a Spiritual Path

237

OU. O-sensei referred to this perfecting of the human spirit as *mizu no tama ga oriru,* the soul of peace descending into the world of human beings. Mizu no tama descending into this world, blown in the eight directions by the winds of adversity, still gives life to young seeds; even the gods must certainly rejoice.

The virtue of I dimension is called *itsukushimi,* or tenderness, the kind of sensitivity required for absolute intimacy. This is the intimacy of selfless activity in the world. In Zen it is called the "perfection of action wisdom," within which all things are done in harmony with the reality of nature.

Playing the perfect note on the flute, composing the perfect symphony, or even being filled with the truth of the universe is not enough. It can never be enough. Only when the four virtues pour forth without self will there be enough. Only then can each moment be the expression of joy and fulfillment.

To realize the highest judgment is to merge with the pure spirit of Omotaru no kami and Ayakashikone no kami, the ki of Hi and Ni. Omotaru is to be perfect and complete as you are. It is constant giving, yet without any experience of deficiency or lack. Ayakashikone combines beauty with the gentle quality of perfect wisdom. Zen master Dogen used the phrase "traceless enlightenment."

In other words, there is nothing here that can be spoken of in terms of obtaining or understanding something. "Rather there should be a gradual getting ourselves out of the way and allowing the true nature of our soul and spirit to fill us. I loaf and invite my soul, I lean and loaf at my ease, observing a spear of summer grass."[14]

This is a state beyond that of the sage or saint. It is called *bonjin,* an ordinary person. There is no smell of holiness or even a hint of perfection. Bonjin, the ordinary person, may perhaps be described as a "free man." In the words of Sakurazawa Nyoichi, "It is one who continually realizes an endless dream."

Life itself is sacred, yet no part of it, including ourselves, is anything special. When we truly grasp this, it is only with a humble and unassuming attitude that we can persevere in our training. "Humility comes in its truest form when one radically understands that there is no reason to be proud."[15]

■ *Itsukushimi, "tenderness"*

■ *Fig. 5.6. Deep meditation of bonjin (from a watercolor by Daniel doAmaral)*

The word for enlightenment in the martial arts is *gokui,* which may be defined as "radical faith." This is not the wish of a frightened beggar; it is a complete trust in this very moment. It is not a belief in anything; it is a belief in everything. The kind of faith that separates one belief or one group of people from another is blind and mistaken and cannot lead toward individual fulfillment or a peaceful world.

The goal must be the embodiment of the absolutely yang ki of Omotaru no kami, endlessly enjoying this life and giving joy to others as well. Our quest began with our ability to ask the question, "What is the truth of reality?" It is resolved in one word. The answer is a resounding I-Ye-Su, the kototama of absolute positivism. In English we would say, "Yes, it is good!"

Inochi: Aikido as a Spiritual Path

APPENDIX ∎ ITSURA

The Fifty Sounds of the Kototama

The secrets of the thirty-two child sounds have been passed down to the Japanese emperor since ancient times as the study of the Kojiki, the Japanese equivalent to the Old Testament of the Bible. In connection with this teaching, there have been, in the last one hundred years or so, a handful of kototama scholars who have also attempted to unravel this ancient mystery.

In Buddhism, the thirty-two child sounds born from *amatsu iwasaka* are called "the thirty-two wishes of Amitabha, the future Buddha." It is said that no one other than a Buddha, or completely realized one, should attempt to explain them. To do so would be to risk premature death. The child sounds explained in this manner, however, comprise a complete description of how they create both mind and body.

Since I am not a realized Buddha, I have attempted to approach this subject from a much less extensive perspective. I've given only a general description of these sounds in an attempt to reveal their spiritual function, and to encourage others to pursue their own spiritual practice without the dualistic illusion of a separate self outside the domain of nature's laws.

In any case, to pass down a description of the thirty-two child sounds is an intellectual endeavor at best. Until each of the sounds is realized and embodied through the experience of actual physical and spiritual training, it cannot truly be transformational. Here then, for the reader's own contemplation, are the fifty sounds in translation.

The Row of A—
Water Ki within the Empty Sky
(Mother sounds, the dimensions of universal ki)

A—Infinite expansion; the first kototama, which gives birth to the essence of Su. All other kototama are born from A. Should be understood as the ki of Heaven. It is Sakitama, the soul of spiritual prosperity and compassion.

I—Center of the center; one point, the life will. This is the absolute here and now (*nakaima*). It is the ultimate source of life, movement, and function. It may be seen as fire, water, or earth ki depending on its circumstances. It is Kushitama, the mysterious soul of enlightenment. It is the virtue of Ame no Minaka Nushi (Su).

U—The universal body; the three-dimensional universe. It is the consciousness of the five senses and absolute unity of body and spirit. It is called *naobi,* the corrective soul from which the other aspects of consciousness are born and ultimately depend.

E—Branching out and cycling ki; the power of judgment. This is fire ki. It is called Aratama, the rough soul, yet it is the only tool of refinement through which I dimension's consciousness can be reached.

O—The ki of continuity and conclusion; the power of memory. It is Nigitama, the soul of love and harmony. Ki-musubi, the tying together of ki leading to the beginning of movement.

The Row of Ta—Fire Ki within Water
(Yang power pushing outward and creating the fullness of each dimension)

Ta—Fire ki within water. The power of contrast; meeting of two electromagnetic energy fields (*atari*).

Pushing out completed word souls from ana into mana, the conscious mind. Square inside a cross.

Ti (chi)—Fire ki within water. The power of wisdom (*prajna*); the fullness of I dimension's ki. The blood, which purifies and sustains the body. *Toku* = the power of melting hardness and solving the mysteries of life. It is called "the unborn ki of both Heaven and Earth." Spirit of the lake.

Tu (tsu)—Water ki within fire. Cycling; power of materialization. The activity of mana appearing in the brain.

Te—(Fire-Water) The power of intellect creating (*shuho*) method, law, and order in nature.

To—Fire ki within water. Fullness of memory; clarity, transparency; unlimited power; enlightenment (*satori*).

The Row of Ki—Fire Ki

Ka—Brightly shining fire ki. Releasing power, the mind begins to move, yet perception is unclear. Symbol is *manji* and cursive cross in circle. See page 48.

Ki—Shaded, hidden light of fire ki. Foundation of life energy, breath, intention.

Ku—Shaded light of fire ki. The spiritual background of A-Wa. The void or empty sky; the working of the three-dimensional universe. Manifesting the activities of Ke.

Ke—Shaded light of fire ki. Judgment based on feeling. Gathering mana together to be judged by Me, the embodiment of E dimension's capacity.

Ko—Shaded light of fire ki. The universal child; completed mana; light wave vibration; materialization of Ki.

The Row of Ma—Water Ki within Fire
(Embodiment of ki, the ki of cycling around and enclosing)

Ma—Water ki within fire. *Makoto,* the pure body of A. Perfect interval; pure spirit. Perfect harmony, circle.

Mi—Water ki within fire. *Mitsu (mizu),* embodiment of threefold essence. Flexible ki, expanding and contracting freely.

Mu—Water ki within fire. The body of A-Wa. *Sunyata,* the first origin; the consciousness of undifferentiated unity, birthplace of both mind and matter. Seen as emptiness, it is existence; seen as existence, it is emptiness. Manifesting the activity of Me as life vibration.

Me—Water ki within fire. Embodiment of the capacity for judgment; eye of judgment. Selecting mana to be expressed as *kana.* Beginning of clarity.

Mo—Water ki within fire. Carrying words' souls over to each other and tying them together for retention. *Ami,* the tying together of the activity of Ta.

The Row of Ha—The Pure Spirit of Fire
(Creative breath—ki—of the universe)

Ha—The power of recognition. Universal vitality reaching out in all directions to the extremities of the universe, where it shines forth as Ki-Ki-Ki. Symbol is the mountain, which represents vibration, and a square with eight directions.

Hi—Pure spirit of fire ki that encircles the heavens. Origin of both in and out breath. The first advent of the will; shining forth brightly, it is the power of enlightenment. The essence of the fourth dimension.

Hu—The breath of separation dividing subject and object. The breath (ki) that gives sound to the silent mana.

He—Fire ki as extension of the activity of Ho. Bringing forth the quality of genius.

Ho—Spiritual origin blazing forth. The maturity and ripeness of pure spirit giving birth to instinctive mind. Its symbol is the peak of the mountain.

The Row of Ra—
Water Ki of Materialization
(Dirty water)

Ra—Yang expanding spiral of spirit. Encompassing mana for actual thought. The final act of creation as Taka Ama Hara.

Ri—Principle; power of pure reason. Tightly contracted spiral.

Ru (Ryu)—The smooth uninterrupted (Su) flow (Ru) of consciousness. Returning to the origin. Figure 4.31 depicts the symbol of Ru.

Re—*Uruwashii,* beauty, grace, elegance. Floating consciousness.

Ro—Slowly revolving spiral of yang ki. Mana entering the brain as the mist of emerging consciousness.

The Row of Na—
The Power of Receiving

Na—Fire-water ki. Birth of the *name;* the mana becomes clear in the brain. This is the constant becoming of clear thought and words. Clarity manifests as the question of existence. *Nani,* what is it?

Ni—Fire-water ki. *Itsukushimi,* benevolence, tenderness. Carrying Hi, the ki of pure spirit.

Nu—Fire-water ki. The materialization of No; the mechanical response of the five senses to outside stimulus. Carrying the spirit without interpretation or confusion.

Ne—Fire-water ki. *Oto,* sound, the root of intellect. The perceived sound is reduced to soundless mana in the brain.

No—Water ki. Extending infinitely and tying things together. This is the descending of Su as instinctive mind, transforming the mana into movement and action.

The Row of Ya—
The Power of Standing in the
Center and Unifying

Ya—Fire-water. Spiritual awakening. Turning one's direction straight toward divine spirit.

Yi—Fire within water. Nakaima, the absolute here and now. Unification of individual will and universal will. In breath.

Yu—Fire within water. Harmony of fire and water. Breath and spirit together like boiling water.

Ye—Fire within water. The perfect judgment reflecting the will of Heaven; giving direction to the activity of Yu.

Yo—Fire-water. The nest (Su) of the fifty sounds (Iwa). *Kaname,* the axis between fire and water ki. Extreme yang ki of nurturing all things.

The Row of Sa—Water Ki Rising
(Power of movement)

Sa—Water ki rising. Opening, blossoming, breaking through. Opening of the ear.

Si—Water ki rising. *Mana,* ruler of the fourth dimension. Our spiritual antennae.

Su—Fire ki within water. Brings the five senses to a state of peace; ruler of the kototama.

Se—Fire ki within water. *Tatewake,* the judgment of the sage; apparent world (*yoko*) judged by the wisdom of spirit (*tate*).

So—Fire-water ki. *Sonen,* ancestors; *moto,* origin.

The Row of Wa—
The Spirit of Water-Fire
(This row deals with Earth. It is objective consciousness, complementing the subjective consciousness of the row of A.)

Wa—Water-fire ki. Saltwater, creating the round form of harmony. No consciousness of the fifty sounds.

Wi—Water-fire ki. The wellspring of life power. The magnetic power that moves the tides and draws energy into its center. The spiritual body of Ame no Minaka Nushi, the kototama of Su.

Wu—Water-fire ki. Spiral of water ki descending like a whirlpool. Balances the floating ki of U; basically indistinguishable in any other way.

We—Water-fire ki. Ki winding around and enclosing. Judgment capacity.

Wo—Water-fire ki. Small self, the end, capacity for memory.

NOTES

CHAPTER 1. AIKITAMA: THE SPIRIT OF UNIVERSAL HARMONY

1. Lama Anagarika Govinda, *Foundations of Tibetan Mysticism* (York Beach, ME: Samuel Weiser, 1969), 58.

2. Manorhita, the twenty-second patriarch of Indian Buddhism.

3. *The Oxford Annotated Bible: The Holy Bible* (New York: Oxford Univ. Press, 1962), 4 (Matthew 5:13).

4. Govinda, *Foundations of Tibetan Mysticism,* 26.

5. Michio Kushi, *The Origin and Destiny of Man,* vol. 2 (Brookline, MA: East West Foundation, 1971), 57.

6. Govinda, *Foundations of Tibetan Mysticism,* 26.

7. Koji Ogasawara, unpublished letters.

8. Jae Jah Noh, *Do You See What I See?* (Wheaton, IL: Quest Books, 1977), 121.

9. Koji Ogasawara, *Kototama Hyakushin,* English edition (Tokyo: Daisan Bunmei Kai, 1973), 7.

10. Kiyoshi Mizutani, ed., *Dai Nippon Shinten* (Nagoya, Japan: n.p., 1907), 10. This volume is in Japanese. Extract translated by William Gleason.

11. Ibid.

12. Govinda, *Foundations of Tibetan Mysticism,* 179.

13. *The Oxford Annotated Bible: The Holy Bible,* 1 (Genesis 1:3).

14. Koji Ogasawara, *Kototama Hyakushin,* 12.

15. Richard Wilhelm and Cary F. Baynes, trans., *The I-Ching or Book of Changes* (Princeton, NJ: Princeton Univ. Press, 1950), 272.

16. Wilhelm and Baynes, *The I-Ching or Book of Changes,* 270.

17. Lao Tzu, *The Complete Works of Lao Tzu,* trans. Hua-Ching Ni (Los Angeles: Sevenstar Communications, 1979), 13.

18. *The Oxford Annotated Bible: The Holy Bible* 1, (Genesis 1:3).

CHAPTER 2. SANGEN: THE UNIQUE PRINCIPLE OF DYNAMIC MONISM

1. Lao Tsu, *Tao Te Ching,* trans. D. C. Lau (Middlesex, UK: Penguin Books, 1963), 49.

2. Michio Kushi and Alex Jack, *The Gospel of Peace* (Tokyo: Japan Publications, 1992), 67.

3. Anzan Hoshin, *Mountains and Rivers: Zen Teachings on the San Sui Kyo of Dogen zenji* (Ottawa, Canada: Great Matter Publications, 1991), 4.

4. Minoru Inaba, *Researching Japanese Budo, Budojo Shiseikan Textbook No. 5* (Tokyo: Meiji Jingu Press, 2006), 66.

5. Yoshio Sugino, quoted in Stanley Pranin, ed., *Aikido Masters* (Tokyo and Henderson, NV: Aiki News, 1993), 206.

6. Noh, *Do You See What I See?,* 13.

CHAPTER 3. IKI: THE BREATH OF LIFE

1. Minoru Inaba, *Researching Japanese Budo,* 49.

CHAPTER 4. SHUGYO: THE SPIRITUAL TRAINING OF TECHNIQUE

1. Minoru Inaba, *Researching Japanese Budo,* 49.

2. Benjamin P. Lo, Martin Inn, Susan Foe, and Robert Amacker, eds., *The Essence of T'ai Chi Ch'uan* (Berkeley, CA: North Atlantic Books, 1979), 19.

3. Ibid., 21.

4. Kisaburo Ohsawa, from author's personal records.

5. Noh, *Do You See What I See?,* 151.

6. Lo, Inn, Foe, and Amacker, *The Essence of T'ai Chi Ch'uan,* 53.

7. Ilza Veith, trans., *The Yellow Emperor's Classic of Internal Medicine* (Berkeley: Univ. of Calif. Press, 2002), 19.

8. R. Buckminster Fuller (Michael Moncur's Quotations, www.quotationspage.com).

9. Noriaki Inoue quoted in Pranin, *Aikido Masters,* 33.

CHAPTER 5. INOCHI: AIKIDO AS A SPIRITUAL PATH

1. Govinda, *Foundations of Tibetan Mysticism,* 149–50.

2. Noh, *Do You See What I See?,* 65.

3. Ibid., 56.

4. Dogen zenji, *Shobogenzo,* book 3, trans. Thomas Cleary (Honolulu: Univ. of Hawai'i Press, 1986), 29.

5. *The Holy Bible: King James Version* (Philadelphia: National Publishing Company, 1978), 1097 (St. John 1:5).

6. Masahilo Nakazono, *Guide to Inochi (Life) Medicine* (Sante Fe, NM: Kototama Institute, 1979), 59.

7. Ibid., 60.

8. Zenzaburo Akazawa, quoted in Pranin, *Aikido Masters,* 273.

9. Po-tuan Chang, *Understanding Reality* (Honolulu: Univ. of Hawai'i Press, 1987), 4.

10. Koji Ogasawara, *Kototama Hyakushin,* 53.

11. Ibid.

12. Hongzhi, *Cultivating the Empty Field: The Silent Illumination of Zen Master Hongzhi,* trans. and ed. Taigen Daniel Leighton (San Francisco: North Point Press, 1991), 28.

13. Hoshin, *Mountains and Rivers,* 4.

14. Walt Whitman, *Leaves of Grass,* 150th anniversary edition (New York: Oxford University Press, 2005), 1.

15. Noh, *Do You See What I See?,* 136.

GLOSSARY

agatsu = Defeating oneself.

ai-hanmi = Matching stance.

aikitama = The spirit of universal harmony.

ai-uchi = Mutual destruction; both sides strike the other at the same time; choosing death in order to live.

ajikan = (Buddhist) "To see with the mind's eye"; meditation on the sacred syllable of A.

Akahitomeso = Mythological princess of the emperor lineage in the age of Fukiaezu.

akuma = The space of evil; the devil.

Ama terasu oh mi kami = Goddess of the sun.

amatsu = That which is contained within heaven; ana, the original consciousness.

amatsu futonorito = Kototama order of AIEOU; highest order of consciousness.

amatsu iwasaka = Seventeen a priori deities in five levels; the contents of Heaven, or ana.

amatsu kanagi = The view of Earth; kototama order of AIUEO.

amatsu sugaso = The view of Heaven; kototama order of AOUEI.

ame (ama) = Heaven; the realm of consciousness.

ame no hashi date = The standing bridge of Heaven.

Ame no Minaka Nushi = The kototama of Su; the creator spirit at the center of Heaven.

ame no nuhoko = The divine spear of Izanagi no kami and Izanami no kami.

ame no uki hashi = The floating bridge of Heaven; kototama beginning with A and U as Heaven and Earth, and finishing with I and Wi as the final receivers of that ki; the cross of tate and yoko, or sometimes tate and nuki.

ana = The heavenly names. *See* amatsu iwasaka.

Aratama = The ki of E and Rei; the kototama of E and Re; the spirit of fire; the rough soul.

arigatai = Feeling of gratitude.

arigatasa = Gratitude.

atemi = A strike or punch.

aum (om) = The sacred syllable that encompasses all spiritual vibrations.

Awaji no Ho no Sawake Shima = U dimension's consciousness from which self-consciousness (A-Wa) occurs; the island of self-consciousness.

Ayakashikone = The root (Ne) of wisdom, reverence, and grace (kashiko) manifest into form (aya).

Ayakashikone no kami = Deity of earth ki; the kototama of Ni.

banyu aigo = Love and caring for all nature and all living things.

bataashi = Stomping the feet.

Boddhisattva-yana = The vehicle of E dimension's consciousness.

bonjin = A simple or ordinary person with purity of heart.

Budo = The martial way of Japan; a shortened form of "Bushido, the way of chivalry."

bunrei = Individual spirit as a division of the universal spirit.

bunryoku = A component of the total force of nature.

chakra = An energy center in the body that relates to the development of higher consciousness.

chi kung = A method of movement and breath coordination designed to strengthen the ki.

chinkon kisshin = Bringing the five senses to a relaxed and peaceful state, and returning to the kototama of Su.

chin na = The Chinese word for gyakute.

chi no kokyu = The breath of Earth.

chuden = Intermediate-level teachings.

de-ai = The initial "coming out" to meet your partner's attack.

dharma = Universal law; the order of the universe.

Dharmakaya = The ground of being.

dojo = Place where michi, the way of life, is practiced.

dotai = The trunk of the body, from the top of the diaphragm down to the legs.

emptiness = In Buddhist terms, the lack of individual or separate being.

Fsu Hi = Mythological Chinese emperor who first interpreted the philosophy of yin and yang.

Fuji = Name of a mountain in Japan; kototama for "no two."

Funakogi = "Boat rowing" exercise for practicing the power of contrast (i.e., balancing the eight powers).

fune = Boat.

Furutama = Misogi practice for centering and bringing ki down to your hara.

futomani = The kototama.

futonorito = Highest order of the fifty sounds (itsura) of the kototama; AIEOU.

gedan = A defensive posture.

geza = The lower seat; hell, the realm of U dimension's consciousness.

gi = Matter.

gnnyaa = The kototama used to express the first cry of an infant.

godan = Fifth-degree black belt rank.

gokui = Highest level of I dimension's consciousness; radical faith; traceless enlightenment.

goryoku = The combination of all forces of nature.

go shiki jin = The five original branches of the human race.

gui (kui) = The bringing together of two elements of spiritual ki.

gyaku hamni = Reverse stance.

gyakute = Jujutsu term meaning "to reverse the joint" (chin na).

hachidan = Eighth-degree black belt rank.

hachiriki = The eight powers; the eight consonants of the kototama; the levels of materialization and human development.

hakaru = To weight something or to determine its value.

handblade = The little finger side (fire ki) of the hand (*tegatana*).

hanmi = Triangle stance.

hanmi handachi = One person standing and the other one seated in seiza.

hara = Origin; the source of ki and blood in our body; our physical and psychic center.

hashi = The horizontal ki of fire; *ha*, "eight," and *shi*, "words."

hataraki = Function, or motive power of hara.

hi = Spirit; light; fire.

higan = The other shore, or enlightenment.

hikari = Light; the running of spirit; invisible light wave vibration.

himitsu (himizu) = Secret; mystery; fire and water ki.

hinayana = In Buddhism, it is the enlightenment of A dimension (*pratyeka-yana*).

hi no ki = Fire ki.

hi no te = The hand of fire.

hiraki = Opening; expanding, or expansion.

hitari (hidari) = The left side.

Hitori gami = An entity that occupies the whole universe by itself and is omnipresent in it; individual deity.

hochi (chi, Shi) = The first particle of spiritual ki.

honno = Instinctive mind.

hou = Law; method; dharma.

ichinen = The momentary spark of perception that occurs within nakaima.

ichirei = Naohi, the universal spirit and our own personal spirit; the spirit of self-correction.

iki = Breath; life; water ki (I) and fire ki (Ki).

iki wo kumu = Tying the breath of life (ki) together.

Ikkajo = Formerly the first category of Aikido techniques.

Ikkyo = The first teaching and technique of Aikido.

Ikugui no kami = The kototama of Mi; the kototama of Rei; the beauty of elegance that leads the E dimension into the I dimension.

inochi = Life; the path of a human being; the path toward I dimension's ki.

inori = Prayer; merging the vibrations of the higher and the lower.

irimi = Entering.

Irimi nage = Entering throw; one of the three main techniques of Aikido.

irimi-tenkan = Entering and turning; the spiral principle of Aikido.

Ise Jingu = The main Shinto shrine in Japan where Ama terasu oh mikami, the goddess of the sun, is enshrined.

ishi no ue ni sannen = "Three years sitting on a rock," a Zen expression describing the proper attitude for the first three years of training.

Isuzu no Kawa = The river of fifty bells at Ise Shrine.

itsukushimi = Tenderness; affection.

itsura = The fifty sounds of the kototama strung together in their natural order.

iwasu = Iwa is the fifty sounds, Su is the nest of the fifty sounds.

iwatsuchi = Sound entering the ear (*tsuchi* = the brain).

Iyo no Futana Shima = *Iyo* (to unite the breath) and *futana* (two names); where Heaven and Earth reunite.

Izanagi no kami and Izanami no kami = Receiving the ki of A and U they become I-Wi, the stabilization and completion of ame no uki hashi, the floating bridge of Heaven; the subjective and objective sides of consciousness.

jiyu jizai = Absolute freedom through self-realization.

jodan hasso = Upper-position sword stance.

joriki = The power of concentration.

judan = Tenth-degree (dan) black belt.

jutai = Techniques based on flexibility.

jutsu = Technique.

kaeshi waza = The reversal of a technique.

kaiten = Cycling.

Kaiten nage = A cycling technique.

kakomu = A square; boundary of the universe.

kama = A cooking pot.

kami = Fire ki (Ka) and water ki (Mi).

kamigakari = To merge with or be possessed by a deity.

Kami musubi no kami = The kototama of Wa; water ki encircling fire ki as in karami.

kamisama = God or deity.

kami waza = The perfection of nature's harmony; divine technique.

kamyo = The age of the gods.

kana = Japanese letters; the names of the gods, which manifest as mana or word souls.

kanagi = The kototama order of AIUEO governing the physical or material view of existence.

kanji = Ideogram.

Kannagara no michi = The ancient name of Shinto; (lit.) the flow of divine consciousness.

Kannon sama = The Boddhisatva Avalokitesvara; the goddess of mercy.

kanro no hou = The sweet nectar of heavenly dew (consciousness).

kara = Empty.

karada = Body.

karami = Winding around, as in fire and water ki (kami) winding around each other.

katana = A sword (*tachi*).

katate tori = A one-handed grasp attack.

kata tori = A shoulder grasp.

katsu hayabi = Instantaneous and complete spiritual awakening.

keiko = The word for a class session; (lit.) to study the mind of the ancients.

Keikyo = Early form of Christianity in China; the divine shining light.

kesa giri = "Cutting the robe," a type of sword cut.

ki = The force of life.

ki-ai = A shout that sometimes accompanies martial movements in order to increase power and effectiveness.

ki-atari = A connection of ki with no gaps between uke and nage.

kihon waza = Basic technique.

ki-musubi = Merging your ki with that of your partner in movement.

kiriage / kiri age = Cutting upward.

kiri oroshi = Cutting downward.

kiru = To cut.

kitai = The techniques of mind over matter; spiritual body.

Kojiki = The book of ancient events, a Japanese book akin to the Old Testament of the Christian Bible.

kokyu = Breath; breathing; expansion-contraction.

Kokyu ho = Exercise for developing kokyu ryoku, the power of kokyu.

Kokyu nage = A throw based solely on the movement of kokyu.

kokyu ryoku = The power of kokyu.

Kokyu undo = Exercise for proper movement in Kokyu ho.

kori = A particle of ki or energy.

kotai = A method of practice for strengthening muscle, bone, and tendons; solid body training.

Kote gaeshi (Kote hineri) = (Lit.) returning the wrist back toward the arm.

kotoha (kotoba) = Words; language.

kototama = Word soul; the spirit of words; mana; the mani jewel, symbolized by prayer beads in Christianity, Buddhism, and Shinto.

kotowari = The principle of the word; pure reason.

kubi shime = A choke hold.

kudan = Ninth-degree black belt.

Kuni toko tachi no kami = Deity representing the kototama of A.

Kushitama = The mysterious soul; the kototama of I and Gi; I dimension's ki.

kuzushi = Unbalancing your partner.

ma-ai = Proper distance.

Mahayana = The great vehicle; the path for the salvation of all sentient beings in Buddhism.

makoto = Sincerity; truth; reality.

mana, manna = Word souls in the subconscious mind.

mani jewel = Symbol of mana; the kototama.

manji = Ancient character for the motive power of the universe; in Sanskrit, sauvastica.

masakatsu = To win directly, correctly, and with integrity.

matomari = Bringing things to a conclusion.

matsuri = To unite Heaven and Earth; a Shinto festival.

men tsuki = Face punch.

michi = The path toward self-realization.

michiru = Fullness; abundance.

miizu = Divine authority of Heaven.

miki (migi) = The right side; the ki of water (mizu no ki).

minaka = Center within the center; exact center.

misogi = Spiritual purification rituals.

mitsu = Essence; the number 3.

mizu = Water.

mizu no ki = The ki of water.

mizu no tama ga oriru = The descending of the spirit of water.

mizu no te = The hand of water.

mono ni narimashita = To become accomplished.

morote tori = Two hands grasping one.

motogaeri = Returning to the origin.

mudra = Hand form for directing one's ki and creating a particular state of mind.

mugamae = Stance of no-stance.

mune tsuki = A punch to the midsection.

musubi = Great unity of matter and spiritual ki.

nage = A throw; a person who throws.

naikan = (Lit.) looking inside; silent meditation.

nakaima = The absolute here and now; axis of time-space.

nanadan = Seventh-degree black belt.

naname = Diagonal; the result of blending tate and yoko.

naohi (naobi) = Our direct and corrective spirit; the essence of individual and universal spirit.

natsukashisa = Nostalgia.

Nestorian = An Indian phrase for an early practice of Christianity.

Ni = The absorbing power of the earth.

nidan = Second-degree black belt.

Nigitama = The soul of harmony.

Nikyo = The second technique.

ninau = To carry (a burden).

ningen = Human being; the space of a human being.

no kami = Translates as "god of."

norito (inori) = Prayer.

nuki = Cross threads in weaving; the weft.

oho = Dai, or greatness.

Ohotonobe no kami = The kototama for Ri. Also the kototama of Gi.

Glossary

250

Ohotonoji no kami = The kototama of Si. Also the kototama of I.

okuden = Advanced or secret teachings.

omoi/omou = Weight; thought.

Omotaru no kami = The kototama of Hi.

omote = Face front; yang; direct opposition; all things revealed.

Onokoro Shima (Onogoro Jima) = The island of self-creation; the original consciousness of mankind.

osae = To hold or force down; to suppress.

osameru = To bring things to a conclusion.

prana (prajna) = Wisdom; breath; ki.

pratyeka-yana = A dimension; in Buddhism, the second stage of enlightenment, the hinayana.

rei = Propriety; example; spirit.

Reiki ho = Original name for Kokyu ho; a practice for developing the power of ki.

reishu, shinju, taizoku = The principle of spirit leading, mind following, and body attached.

reitai ittai = Spirit and body as one.

renshu = Repetitive practice.

ryokudan = Sixth-degree black belt.

ryote tori = Grasping both of your partner's arms.

ryutai = Flowing technique; practical Aikido techniques.

Sakitama (Sachitama) = The soul of prosperity; the kototama of A.

sampeki = The dragon that comes out of the east.

sandan = Third-degree black belt.

sangen = The three origins; the principle of aiki, or universal harmony.

sankaku ho − The triangle method.

Sankyo = The third technique.

satori = Enlightenment; to remove the difference.

Sa means "difference" and *tori* means "to take away" or "remove."

sattvas = The five vehicles of Buddhism.

Sattva-yana = The vehicle of the body; U dimension's consciousness.

sauvastica = Ancient symbol of motive power. Also called manji.

sawake = Slight difference or separation; a slight opening.

seishi kami ichimai = "The difference between life and death is the thickness of a sheet of paper."

seishin = Individual character or mental countenance.

seiza = Sitting formally on one's knees.

sensen no te = Moving first, after your partner's intention is already set on attack.

sente = Taking the initiative.

sente no nai budo = Martial art that doesn't attack first.

Shiho nage = Four-directions throw.

shikaku = A square; (lit.) four corners; competency; qualification.

shikon = The four souls.

shima (jima) = An island; an enclosure of the mind.

shimeru = To enclose; to be immersed.

shin = Faith.

Shingon Mikkyo = Esoteric Buddhist sect; secret teaching of the true word.

shinju = *See* reishu.

shin kokyu = Deep, spiritual breathing.

shinreikai = The divine spiritual world; ana; amatsu iwasaka.

shinshin toitsu = Unification of body, mind, and ki.

shizentai = A natural stance, mugamae.

shizuka (shisuka) = Quietness.

shizumeru = To settle down; to come to a state of peace.

Shobu = Martial art for the development of wisdom.

shodan = First-degree black belt.

shomen uchi = An overhand strike to the center of the forehead; cutting downward.

shugyo = Spiritual training.

sonen = The level of consciousness below the subconscious; the original place of thought and feeling; ancestors.

souzou = To create; to contemplate.

sravaka-yana = The first stage of enlightenment; going beyond the idea of a personal soul or self.

subayaka = Light and swift; speedy movement.

suberu = The spiral principle of universal order and control; the way of governing without force.

sugaso = Kototama in the order of AOUEI.

Suhijini no kami = The kototama of Yi; the kototama of Su.

sujimichi = A pattern of thought; logic; a spiritual path; michi.

suki = A weak point or opening where one can be struck.

sumo = The Japanese national sport of wrestling.

sunyata = The clear mirror of perfect mind.

suriashi = Sliding the feet lightly over the mat as you move forward swiftly, with the large toe in line with the shinbone.

suwari waza = Techniques done on the knees.

Ta = The power of contrast (*tata no chikara*).

tai-atari = Whole body contact; direct collision of force.

taikyoku = The absolute.

tai-sabaki = Body movement as an expression of judgment.

Taka Ama Hara = The high heavenly plane.

Takami musubi no kami = The kototama of A.

takemusu = The process of creation through the blending of yin and yang factors.

tama = A perfect sphere; spirit; soul.

tamashihi = Our individual soul.

tanagokoro = The palm of the hand; the heart, or hara, in the hand.

tanden = Another word for hara.

tanden no ichi = One point; the center of hara.

tareru = Hanging down.

taru = To be sufficient.

tate = Vertical; standing; the main thread in weaving.

ten = Heaven.

tenchi nage = Let; Heaven-Earth throw; a kokyu nage in which ki is sent up and down simultaneously.

ten-jin-chi = Heaven, man, and Earth as the three components of reality.

ten no kokyu = The breath of Heaven.

Ti = The original spark of life.

toku = The power of melting hardness and solving the mysteries of life.

tono = Lord; ruler.

To-Su = Passing through.

Toyokumu no kami = The kototama of O.

tsuchi no ki = Earth ki; the ki of the center.

tsuki = A thrust or straight punch.

tsunagu = To tie (the ki) together.

Tsunugui no kami = The kototama of Ki. Also representing the kototama of E as the opening of spiritual vision.

Uhijine no kami = The kototama of Ti; the kototama of U.

uke = Receiver.

ukemi = The art of falling; the art of receiving.

uki = The floating ki of the universe.

uku = To float.

umi = The ocean from which physical life is born on this planet.

umu = The power of birth.

undo = Exercise.

ura = The back side; yin, evasive movement; entering behind your partner.

uruwashisa = Beauty; grace; elegance; the qualities of a Boddhisattva.

ushiro = The back side; an attack from behind.

utsushiyo = The manifest world as a reflection of the world of ki.

wabi sabi = The essence of timeless antiquity manifest here and now.

wake = To separate or divide.

ware = Divided self.

ware soku uchu = Saying of Morihei Ueshiba that translates as "The universe and myself are the same."

Ya = The beginning of self-consciousness; opening the eye of Heaven.

yana = Vehicle.

Yata no Kagami = The sacred mirror within Ise Jingu, the main shrine of Japan.

Yellow Emperor = Mythological emperor of ancient China.

yoko = Side; horizontal.

yokomen uchi = A strike to the side of the head.

yondan = Fourth-degree black belt.

Yonkyo = Fourth teaching.

zanshin = Continuing concentration.

BIBLIOGRAPHY

Deguchi, Onisaburo. *Michi no Shiori*. Tokyo: O-moto Kyo, 1948 [in Japanese].

———. *Reikai Monogatari*. Tokyo: Tentei Publications, Showa 33, 1992 [in Japanese].

Dogen zenji. *Shobogenzo*. Translated by Thomas Cleary. Honolulu: Univ. of Hawai'i Press, 1986.

Govinda, Lama Anagarika. *Foundations of Tibetan Mysticism*. York Beach, ME: Samuel Weiser, 1969.

The Holy Bible: King James Version. Philadephia: National Publishing Company, 1978.

Hongzhi. *Cultivating the Empty Field: The Silent Illumination of Zen Master Hongzhi*. Translated and edited by Taigen Daniel Leighton. San Francisco, CA: North Point Press, 1991. Paperback reissue, Boston, Rutland, VT, and Tokyo: Tuttle Press, 2000.

Hoshin, Anzan. *Mountains and Rivers: Zen Teachings on the San Sui Kyo of Dogen zenji,* 2nd rev. ed. Ottawa, Canada: Great Matter Publications, White Wind Zen Community, 1991.

Inaba, Minoru. *Researching Japanese Budo, Budojo Shiseikan Textbook No. 5*. Tokyo: Meiji Jingu Press, 2006.

Kushi, Michio. *The Origin and Destiny of Man,* vol. 2. Brookline, MA: East West Foundation, 1971.

Kushi, Michio, and Alex Jack. *The Gospel of Peace*. Tokyo: Japan Publications, 1992.

Lao Tsu. *Tao Te Ching*. Translated by D. C. Lau. London: Penguin Classics, 1964.

Lao Tzu. *The Complete Works of Lao Tzu*. Translated by Hua-Ching Ni. Los Angeles: Sevenstar Communications, 1979.

Lo, Benjamin P., Martin Inn, Susan Foe, and Robert Amacker, eds. *The Essence of T'ai Chi Ch'uan*. Berkeley, CA: North Atlantic Books, 1979.

Mizutani, Kiyoshi, ed. *Dai Nippon Shinten*. Nagoya, Japan: n.p., 1979 [in Japanese].

Nakazono, Masahilo. *Guide to Inochi (Life) Medicine*. Sante Fe, NM: Kototama Institute, 1979.

———. *The Kototama Principle*. Sante Fe, NM: The Kototama Institute, 1984.

Noh, Jae Jah. *Do You See What I See?* Wheaton, IL: Quest Books, 1977.

Ogasawara, Koji. *Kototama Hyakushin,* English ed. Tokyo: Daisan Bunmei Kai, 1973.

———. *Kototama Hyakushin,* Japanese ed. Tokyo: Daisan Bunmei Kai, Showa 44, 1973.

The Oxford Annotated Bible: The Holy Bible. New York: Oxford Univ. Press, 1962.

Pranin, Stanley, ed. *Aikido Masters*. Tokyo and Henderson, NV: Aiki News Publishing, 1993.

Saito, Morihiro. *Traditional Aikido.* 5 vols. Tokyo: Minato Research & Publishing Co. Ltd., 1974 [in Japanese and English].

Shi Ming, with Siao Weija. *Mind Over Matter.* Translated by Thomas Cleary. Berkeley, CA: Frog Books, 1994.

Ueshiba, Morihei. *Takemusu Aiki.* Tokyo: Byakko Society, Showa 51, 1976 [in Japanese].

Veith, Ilza, trans. *The Yellow Emperor's Classic of Internal Medicine.* Berkeley: Univ. of California Press, 2002.

Whitman, Walt. *Leaves of Grass*, 150th anniversary edition. New York: Oxford Univ. Press, 2005.

Wilhelm, Richard, and Cary F. Baynes, trans. *The I-Ching or Book of Changes.* Princeton, NJ: Princeton Univ. Press, 1950.

Yamaguchi, Shido. *Kototama Hissho.* Tokyo: Shohan Hakko, 1992 [in Japanese].

INDEX

Page numbers in *italic* indicate figures.

BOOKS OF RELATED INTEREST

The Spiritual Foundations of Aikido
by William Gleason

The Spiritual Practices of the Ninja
Mastering the Four Gates to Freedom
by Ross Heaven

Martial Arts Teaching Tales of Power and Paradox
Freeing the Mind, Focusing Chi, and Mastering the Self
by Pascal Fauliot

Shaolin Qi Gong
Energy in Motion
by Shi Xinggui

Iron Shirt Chi Kung
by Mantak Chia

Bone Marrow Nei Kung
Taoist Techniques for Rejuvenating the Blood and Bone
by Mantak Chia

Nei Kung
The Secret Teachings of the Warrior Sages
by Kosta Danaos

The Magus of Java
Teachings of an Authentic Taoist Immortal
by Kosta Danaos

INNER TRADITIONS • BEAR & COMPANY
P.O. Box 388
Rochester, VT 05767
1-800-246-8648
www.InnerTraditions.com

Or contact your local bookseller